AMAZE

EVERY CUSTOMER

EVERY TIME

PRAISE FOR
AMAZE EVERY CUSTOMER EVERY TIME

"At Zappos, we aim to deliver WOW through service. This book illustrates how important it is to WOW and AMAZE every customer every time!"
— Tony Hsieh, *New York Times* bestselling author of *Delivering Happiness* and CEO of Zappos.com, Inc.

"The message is clear and the lessons are simple. This book is a guide to creating customer loyalty, employee engagement, and overall business success."
— Horst Schulze, former president, Ritz-Carlton Hotels, and chairman/CEO, Capella Hotel Group

"The best way to improve the customer experience is to improve the employee experience. While this book has many great ideas that focus on the customer, Hyken also emphasizes the importance of the internal culture of a company. He perfectly makes this point in the tenth 'tool' of the book, which states that to be the best place to buy, you have to be the best place to work."
— Vala Afshar, chief marketing officer and chief customer officer, Enterasys

"Refreshingly simple, Shep's latest work offers a comprehensive collection of tools and tactics to engage the hearts and minds of employees as a means of engaging and amazing customers."
— Claire Burns, senior vice president and chief customer officer, MetLife

"A cowboy can't be all hat and no horse; a business can't be all product and no service. In *Amaze Every Customer Every Time*, Shep saddles up and showcases the authenticity of Ace Hardware's legendary service. Proving that great service is not in what you do; it has to be ingrained in who you are."
— Jeffrey Hayzlett, global business celebrity, bestselling author, and sometime cowboy

"Thank you for this AMAZING wake-up call! I can't wait for our agents to read this book and take your customer-centric ideas to heart. Our focus is to nurture long-term relationships and create a one-stop shop for real estate needs. We want to 'own our mile!'"
—Tom Meyer, founder and president, Condo 1

"Everyone wants more customers. But the best way to get them is to amaze the ones you already have. And this book shows you exactly how to do that."
—Randy Gage, author of the *New York Times* bestseller
Risky Is the New Safe

"*Amaze Every Customer Every Time* gives you the why, what, and how of amazing customer service. In this highly useful book, Hyken makes it easy to understand and deliver the kind of service that keeps customers coming back for more."
—Mark Sanborn, bestselling author of *The Fred Factor* and
You Don't Need a Title to be a Leader

"It is crystal clear from the onset that this book is not meant to be read. It is meant to be used. This is a how-to book that takes the reader on a compelling journey to the mountaintop of customer service, which Hyken refers to as *Amazement*."
—Benjamin Ola Akande, Ph.D., dean, Webster University,
Walker School of Business & Technology

"As the franchisor of multiple concepts I recognize how important customer service is to the success of a business. This book provides the tools that are needed to create a level of customer service that is . . . Amazing!"
—Dina Dwyer-Owens, chairperson and CEO of
The Dwyer Group

Books by Shep Hyken

Moments of Magic:
Be a Star with Your Customers and Keep Them Forever

The Loyal Customer:
A Lesson from a Cab Driver

Only the Best on Success (coauthor)

Only the Best on Customer Service (coauthor)

Only the Best on Leadership (coauthor)

The Winning Spirit (coauthor)

Inspiring Others to Win (coauthor)

The Cult of the Customer: Create an Amazing Experience
That Turns Satisfied Customers into Customer Evangelists

The Amazement Revolution: Seven Customer Service Strategies
to Create an Amazing Customer (and Employee) Experience

Amaze Every Customer Every Time: 52 Tools for Delivering
the Most Amazing Customer Service on the Planet

For more information about the above books, contact:

Shepard Presentations, LLC
(314) 692-2200
info@hyken.com
www.hyken.com

AMAZE

EVERY CUSTOMER

EVERY TIME

52 TOOLS *for* Delivering
the Most Amazing
Customer Service *on the* Planet

SHEP HYKEN

GREENLEAF
BOOK GROUP PRESS

Published by Greenleaf Book Group Press
Austin, Texas
www.gbgpress.com

Distributed by Greenleaf Book Group LLC

Design and composition by Greenleaf Book Group. Cover design by Greenleaf Book Group. Cover and interior illustration: © Andrew Johnson, 2013. Used under license from iStockphoto LP.

Publisher's Cataloging-In-Publication Data
(Prepared by The Donohue Group, Inc.)
ISBN 13: 978-1-62634-009-1

Hyken, Shep.
  Amaze every customer every time : 52 tools for delivering the most amazing customer service on the planet / Shep Hyken.

    p. ; cm.

  Issued also as an ebook.
  ISBN: 978-1-62634-009-1

  1. Customer services. 2. Consumer satisfaction. 3. Employee empowerment. 4. Corporate culture. 5. Success in business. I. Title.

HF5415.5 .H95 2013
658.8/12   2013931924

Part of the Tree Neutral® program, which offsets the number of trees consumed in the production and printing of this book by taking proactive steps, such as planting trees in direct proportion to the number of trees used: www.treeneutral.com

Special Edition Printing ISBN: 978-1-62634-037-4

Printed in the United States of America on acid-free paper

13 14 15 16 17 18   10 9 8 7 6 5 4 3 2 1

First Edition

CONTENTS

PART ONE

AMAZEMENT 101

"It is not the employer who pays the wages. Employers only handle the money. It is the customer who pays the wages."

—HENRY FORD

A CUSTOMER-CENTERED CULTURE doesn't happen by accident. It happens because of the influence and the conscious choices of the people in the organization. How do you make it purposeful? How do you live the culture you want to create on a daily basis? The answer is: By working on the culture before you work on anything else.

CHAPTER ONE

INTRODUCTION TO AMAZEMENT

Amazing Every Customer Every Time will give you a competitive edge in any economy and any marketplace.

WHAT IS AMAZEMENT, and why should you bother learning what it takes to Amaze Every Customer Every Time?

Amazement is the level of customer experience that gives you a clear advantage in any economy and any marketplace. Amazement is the competitive edge that separates good companies from truly *great* companies. And believe it or not, an amazing customer experience is well within your capacity to deliver to every customer, every single time.

Amazement is the advantage that makes the competition start thinking about how "unfair" it is to have to be operating in the same market, the same planet, the same dimension as you do.

Amazement is what makes it easy for you to stand out and win repeat business, create customer evangelists, and reap referrals—whether times are good or bad; whether your company sells ballpoint pens, ball bearings, or ballroom dancing lessons; whether your customers are consumers, businesses, or both.

Amazement is what the "best of the best" companies have figured out. And it's what you can figure out too. These companies know that no matter how great their product or service, they can't expect to get and keep customers if they don't deliver an amazing experience. Guess what! You can't either.

These companies know what amazement is (and isn't), and they know how to make it happen. And before too long, if you keep turning pages, you will too.

Here's something else the best of the best have figured out: They know that when it comes to delivering truly amazing customer service, everyone in the organization must step up and be a leader. That's true of the best of the best service organizations. And it's true of your organization too.

Amazing Every Customer Every Time doesn't take a specific title. It takes the willingness to step up and become a role model who sets an example that others aspire to. You can do that, right now, whether you founded the company or just got hired today.

HOW TO USE THIS BOOK

We shift gears now to discuss how to best use this book. A lot of business books are meant to be read. This is *not* one of them.

Yes, you heard me right. *This book is not meant to be read.* It is meant to be used!

The next three chapters will give you the "lay of the land" about why I chose Ace Hardware as my role model for this book; why I picked this company to showcase these 52 best practices, tactics, and strategies about how to Amaze Every Customer Every Time. Chapter five, titled "The Seven Amazement Principles," gives you a little bit of background on the vocabulary and key concepts you will find throughout the book.

After that, you're off to the races. The rest of the book—most of it in fact—is divided into five main chapters, which happen to be the five areas that Ace has focused on since 1924 to grow and sustain its business through incredibly difficult economic and competitive times. These strategic areas are leadership, culture, one-on-one customer engagements, gaining a competitive edge, and community. Within these five chapters you will find 52 Amazement Tools in the form of tactics that will help you achieve a specific amazement objective. Some of these tools may appear to be common sense—but unfortunately, common sense is not always so common. Some of them will probably confirm that what you are already doing is on the right track. Others will introduce you to new tactics that you'll want to introduce to your organization. Some can be implemented immediately, while others will take time.

As you start to get into the 52 tools, there are two ways to approach this book.

Some of you will continue reading every page, in order, until you reach the last page of the book, taking notes along the way and deciding how to implement the most relevant tactics throughout.

And others will want more immediate gratification. That's fine. Simply leaf through part two until you find something that catches your eye. While all of the tools are important and useful, there may be one or two that stand out as particularly relevant to your organization and that you feel should get implemented immediately.

Either way, you're supposed to find something that you want to use… and then start using it!

In the chapter titled "Leadership," you'll realize that everyone can take a leadership position and be an amazement role model. While the tactics work for those who hold management responsibilities, don't be fooled into thinking that your title and responsibility doesn't connect to the word "management." When it comes to amazing your customers, everyone can be a leader.

In the chapter titled "Culture," you will find tactics that connect to building a strong service-driven culture. Everyone has their hand in building and sustaining a culture that delivers amazement to both customers and employees.

In the chapter titled "One-on-One," you will get specific tactics that you can use during real-time interactions with individual customers.

In the chapter titled "The Competitive Edge," you'll learn how to take your organization far above the competition by delivering amazing customer service.

And finally, in the chapter titled "Community," you'll learn about building stronger connections with all those people in the larger world with whom you live, and maybe even sell to.

So get started. Read through the chapters in part one. Then, even if you feel compelled to read the rest of the book in its entirety, I urge you to first browse through part two. Find what's relevant and most interesting to you and to your organization, and resolve to implement it.

By the way, at the end of each chapter in part one, each tool in part two, and the epilogue, you will find some summary points under Your Amazement Toolbox. Feel free to quote them at your next meeting, use them as a conversation starter, or tweet them on Twitter to the rest of the world. And at the end of each of the 52 tools and the epilogue, you'll find questions—called The Drill—to help you *drill* deeper into the tactics and implement them better. Make your way through the book in the sequence that makes the most sense to you. Then go back to the beginning of part two to read and start implementing the rest of the strategies and tactics. It only takes one great idea to transform your business!

CHAPTER TWO

THE CASE FOR ACE

Recognized for customer service and being the most helpful stores on the planet, Ace is a perfect role model for amazement.

WHY WRITE A BOOK about Ace Hardware?

Well, first and foremost, let me clarify. This is actually a business book about how to Amaze Every Customer Every Time. So the question is, why choose Ace for such a book? Because I wanted to feature one company as a role model throughout, a single company that exemplifies every current best practice for customer amazement. I looked at all kinds of companies, and I realized that Ace not only fit the bill but also was uniquely positioned as the perfect company to serve as a role model.

Why?

Because you are Ace!

I know that may sound like a strange claim, but read on and see whether you agree with me by the time you get to the end of this chapter.

• • •

Let me begin by saying that I'm a lucky guy. I've been fortunate enough to make a living as a public speaker and consultant on the topic of customer service since the early 1980s. You may remember, depending on how old you are, this was the period when customer service was just beginning to come into vogue as an important subject for business leaders.

And I have seen a whole lot come and go in that time. Three decades ago, we had certain brands and certain companies that stood out as being the true "rock-stars" when it came to building customer loyalty and market dominance.

The "rock-star" brands of that time, the ones best known for their superior customer service, were companies like IBM, Delta Airlines, and Eastman Kodak.

Let's think about this for a minute. IBM is still around, and it is still one of the most successful, most admired companies in America. If it no longer stands out the way it once did as one of the top few service companies in the country, it may be because its market has changed in ways that were impossible for anyone to predict, and because its level of visibility has changed too. In the areas in which it competes, IBM maintains a strong reputation for customer satisfaction that is worthy of its proud history, but it's not the global rock-star brand for customer service that it was during the 1980s. In other words, there are not as many businesses today trying to emulate IBM as there used to be.

Delta Airlines is still up and running, but ask yourself: How many people now look to that airline as a shining, reliable example of great customer service? I believe there's really only one rock-star airline in America right now, and it's not Delta. (It's Southwest Airlines.) In the years since its glory period, Delta has gone through a bankruptcy, and like a lot of the big carriers, it has some ill will to deal with in its customer base. Let's be frank. Most of the airline industry is struggling in terms of its customer satisfaction levels—and just about everything else.

What about Eastman Kodak? Well, something went off track somewhere along the line, and in 2012, it filed for Chapter 11 bankruptcy protection. So you probably can't consider it a rock-star customer service company anymore.

My point is that what's trendy, what's sexy, and what's "hot" is not always a good indicator of a company's long-term philosophy about its customers, or its ability to deliver on that philosophy. It is not necessarily a good role model for the rest of us. Some companies get hot for a while, then seem to cool off, and maybe even go out of business. Meanwhile, other companies with far longer, more impressive, and more relevant records of performance get ignored.

Today, if you asked 100 businesspeople to name the top customer service companies in the country, most of them would name the rock stars of today. They'd name companies like:

Apple

Southwest Airlines

Ritz-Carlton

Nordstrom's

Amazon.com

Those are today's "sexy" customer service companies, and don't get me wrong, they're all doing a great job. My only question would be: How do we know which ones are likely to still be doing a great job 30 years from now?

What if we thought about a different kind of rock star in the arena of customer service and business success?

What if we could identify a company that has consistently been on the right track philosophically, and successfully executing according to that philosophy, for the last 70 or 80 years? What if we went looking for a company that's been offering "proof of concept" on its commitment to customer service by winning just about every customer service award possible for the better part of a century? What if we could find a company that delivered on a brand promise so powerful that it was able to compete—and win—in one of the toughest sectors of our economy, against industry players with far more money to spend?

Well, if we did that, we'd end up face-to-face with a new kind of rock star in the world of customer service—one that might not have as much glitz and media buzz but had a much better chance than anyone else out there of sharing strategies that were relevant today and tomorrow, for companies big and small. We'd be looking at a company that had succeeded in building amazement into the DNA of the business.

We'd be looking at Ace Hardware, which is not only an undiscovered rock star after about 89 years on tour (as of this writing) but also *solid as a rock*. Year in and year out, decade after decade and generation after generation, this brand has stood the test of time, which counts for a lot in my book. And since that's what you happen to be reading, let me tell you some things you might not know about Ace.

YOU KNOW ACE . . .
BUT DO YOU REALLY KNOW ACE?

If you are reading these words, you almost certainly have some history with Ace Hardware. As of this writing, there are more than 4,600 Ace Hardware stores in over 70 countries. I bet you've been in at least one of them, and I bet you've seen plenty of Ace commercials on TV. It's such a familiar part of the landscape, in fact, that you probably think you know Ace Hardware.

But I'll bet you don't.

I'll bet you didn't know that, with the exception of 85 of the 4,600 stores, they are all locally owned and operated. The person who owns and runs that Ace store in your neighborhood is a member of your community. He or she pays taxes to the same local government you do, sends kids to the same schools you do, and votes at the same polling stations you do.

I'll bet you didn't know that each one of those locally owned stores is part of a multibillion-dollar buying group.

And I'll bet that you didn't know that Ace is one of the national leaders in customer satisfaction across all sectors. You may not even have known that Ace is the clear leader in customer satisfaction in the brutally competitive retail hardware sector—and has been for years.

Just so you can get some clarity about the level of achievement I'm talking about here, take a look at this announcement from J.D. Power and Associates, the leading US market research firm in the area of customer satisfaction, product quality, and buyer behavior:

> Ace Hardware Ranks Highest in Customer Satisfaction among
> Home Improvement Retailers for a Sixth Consecutive Year. Ace
> Hardware performs particularly well in the two most influential
> factors: staff and service and store facility.[1]

So now you know: I'm not making this up. Even though this company often flies "under the radar," Ace has been identified as No. 1 in customer service, year after year, in a highly competitive industry—retail hardware—by the top research firm in the country. And there are plenty of other sources that have given Ace this kind of ranking for years. According to a recent *Bloomberg Businessweek* report, Ace ranks in the top ten among *all* US brands for customer satisfaction. That means Ace is hanging with names like Apple Inc., L.L. Bean, and the Four Seasons luxury hotel chain.

Clearly, the people at Ace are doing something right. If you're curious about what that "something right" might be—and whether it could possibly be relevant to your company—read on.

DAVID AND GOLIATH

Over the past year or so, a lot of people have asked me what the follow-up volume to my *New York Times* bestseller *The Amazement Revolution* was going to be. I have to tell you, when I told people it was going to be about Ace Hardware, I got some strange looks. Not only that, I got a lot of puzzled follow-up questions, most of them variations on "At this point in your career, you could write about any company you want . . . so why in the world would you choose to write a book about a hardware store?"

There are a lot of possible answers to that question: I've personally gotten great service from Ace for many years. It's an underappreciated brand. It has stood the test of time. And so on. But my favorite answer of all has only three words: *David and Goliath.*

---

1   J.D. Power and Associates press release, May 4, 2011.

Let me explain what I mean by that. According to the experts, the retail sector seems to be going in one direction: super-big stores that descend on major population centers with low, low pricing as one of their major strategies. Think of the most recognizable players: Walmart, Sam's Club, Office Depot, and so on: big boxes and heavy discounts.

That's the model that hardware competitors like Lowe's and Home Depot are betting the big dollars on. Each of them is committed to building a big company with a centralized command structure that offers consumers big inventory, big floor plans, big parking lots, and big discounts—so the company can win the hard-earned dollar of the consumer who wants the lowest possible price and the widest possible selection of home improvement products.

Isn't "big is better" the mantra now? Isn't that the "new normal" in which the retail sector is supposed to be operating? Most of the experts would say "Yes." If you were betting and asked the experts for advice on the smartest bet, they would tell you to bet on Goliath to beat David, every time.

So, if those are the rules this industry is supposed to be playing by— and a lot of smart people tell us that those *are* the rules—what would *you* bet the marketplace would do to a player like Ace? After all . . .

Ace offers competitive pricing, but typically *doesn't* offer consumers the lowest possible price.

Ace, in almost every location, has *no* huge stores or supersized parking lots.

Ace's stores (as I've mentioned) are almost all *locally owned and operated*—some of them far removed from major population centers. In the 21st-century retail sector, that's an anachronism! You don't typically bet on smaller, locally owned stores (outlets that some might consider "mom-and-pop" stores) to beat the big chains!

If it were your hard-earned money you were betting with—and you'd never seen this book—you'd agree with the experts. Go ahead, admit it. If it were your money, you'd bet that Ace would get beaten, and beaten badly, by these bigger stores with bigger advertising and marketing budgets. That's what most people I talk to predict when I ask them this question.

Here's the reality. Consumers have become extremely price sensitive. They are skeptical and conservative, because everyone in retail is promising great service, but very few retailers are actually delivering anything that can persuade consumers to make buying decisions based on anything besides price. Yet in 2011, a year when the retail sector as a whole was struggling to adapt to this newly price-sensitive consumer, Ace somehow grew its revenues at a much faster rate than its big-box, discount-driven competitors.

Lowe's grew annual revenues by 2.9 percent, Home Depot by 3.5 percent. And Ace? Our under-the-radar rock star grew revenues by 5.1 percent. For what it's worth, Ace also outpaced both of those huge competitors in terms of employee growth during the same period. You can check the numbers for yourself; they're all out there.[2]

How did David beat Goliath?

• • •

My answer starts with a disclaimer. Yes, I know that not every Ace Hardware store always executes 100 percent on the best practices they're supposed to execute on.

You know what, though? I don't really care about that.

Why not? Because I'm not at all that interested in what happens in a small *minority* of the Ace stores.

I'm interested in what happens in *most* of the Ace stores, because in those exemplary stores lies the answer to the question of how David beat Goliath. I'm interested in which company is still going to be around 30, 40, even 50 or more years from now. I want to know which strategies for building customer satisfaction and loyalty are working right now and are built for the long haul—for big businesses, small businesses, and everybody in between.

That's why I picked Ace. It has demonstrated over and over again— in fact, for nearly a century now—that it lives by, operationalizes, and

---

2   See Yahoo! Finance and The Home Depot annual report.

evangelizes a powerful, customer-focused and helpful culture that's built for the long haul.

Ace has built into its operation that customer-focused culture so well that it is capable of delivering higher-than-industry customer loyalty across its whole network of stores. That means Ace is building and supporting a customer-focused culture on the vast scale of a major global brand (which Ace is), and it also means Ace is creating and maintaining that customer-focused culture on the small scale of a local independently owned business.

Ace has been beating Goliath for decades. Its secret for doing so is vitally important to anyone who has competition.

● ● ●

How do you survive and thrive in an industry where your competitors are outspending you on a regular basis? Ace has figured that out.

And you know what else? Ace has figured out an answer to that question that is just as accessible to the strategic leaders of major global brands as it is to a network of local entrepreneurs. This culture is custom-built for people who want to compete—and win—in business. Having worked with Ace for many years now as both a consultant and a speaker, I can tell you that this culture is not only custom-built for a diverse group of local hardware store owners; it is also custom-built for *you*.

YOU ARE ACE.

You may not have realized it, but you are Ace, and here's why:

Ace is a successful small, medium, and large business—simultaneously.

Ace is primarily locally owned and operated by independent business owners . . . and it is also driven by core standards and practices that are set by headquarters.

> Ace is a local community-driven brand . . . and it is also a global multibillion-dollar brand.
>
> Ace is a business-to-consumer brand . . . and a business-to-business brand.

So, what does that mean to you?

> If you are a solo entrepreneur with just one or two employees, it means you will find in this book the right recipe for building a customer-focused business.
>
> If you are small- or medium-sized business, it means you will find in these pages the right recipe for building a customer-focused company.
>
> And if you are part of a larger national or international brand, it means you will also find here the right recipe for your customer-focused organization.

You are Ace!

Can you imagine every Apple store being locally owned? That's the kind of company we'll be looking at in this book. A company that's big, small, and every size in between. A company that's built up powerful customer loyalty that transcends narrow price positioning. A cutting-edge company that's been executing successfully on a powerful promise—and winning rave reviews from its customers and its network of owners—for 85 years.

How do they do it? I'll give you a hint. *They win on people.*

Most of us in business today need to take a closer look at the neglected art of winning on people. Sometimes we can't offer the lowest price. Sometimes we can't deploy the biggest advertising and promotional budget. Sometimes we don't have the biggest inventory. We might not win on any or all of those things, but we can win on amazement, which means winning on people.

Ace wins on *people*. Ace wins on *amazement*. Delivering on amazement in the marketplace is all about caring about the people inside your company: supporting them on the inside and helping them to deliver on the outside. If you are ready and willing to find a way to create loyalty in the marketplace based on the amazement of the customer experience you deliver, if you're willing to bet on David beating Goliath, then congratulations! You are Ace. And I wrote this book for you.

So far, you've read about some of the great things Ace is doing. I have written this book to show you exactly how to do those kinds of great things in your own company, whatever its size, so that you, too, can win in the marketplace and outgrow your competitors—even if they have been around a lot longer than you have, or have more customers than you do, or have thirty times as much to spend on marketing as you do.

If that's what you're here for, you've come to the right place. You are about to learn how to . . .

AMAZE Every Customer Every Time!

YOUR AMAZEMENT TOOLBOX

- Rock-star brands may come and go, but brands that are "rock solid" stay around.

- Ace Hardware is not a franchise. It is a network of privately owned stores.

- Ace is a national leader in customer service across all business sectors, not just hardware.

- According to a recent *Business Week* report, Ace Hardware ranks in the top ten among all US brands for customer satisfaction.

- Even though big-box competitors outspend Ace in advertising by as much as 30-to-1, Ace beats these competitors in revenue growth.

- Ace lives by, operationalizes, and evangelizes a powerful, customer-focused culture that's built for the long haul.

- Ace wins on people and on amazement. Delivering amazement in the marketplace is all about caring for the people inside your company.

CHAPTER THREE

PEOPLE WITH THE PASSION TO SERVE

What do you stand for? What's important to you? Whatever it is, that's what you want to be known for.

SO, ACE IS NOT JUST a successful global brand but also a successful small business: almost every store is locally owned and operated. All of the stores I spent time with were notable for the presence of people who *wanted* to be there. People who loved doing what they were doing. People who had a passion to serve.

How awesome is that?

In the last chapter, I showed you why I believe Ace's record of success in the marketplace, and particularly its long history of competing successfully against much larger, better-capitalized competitors, makes it a great role model for start-ups, family businesses, and global brands alike. You may not have realized how much you had in common with this company—which is both big and small; which is engaged in both business-to-business and business-to-consumer; which is both locally entrepreneurial and centrally managed—but now you know: Ace touches a lot more bases than you may have thought.

In this chapter, I want to show you why you want to be Ace, regardless of what business you happen to be in.

Ace is a new kind of corporate rock star: a top-tier competitor that is solid as a rock because of its demonstrated ability, for nearly a century, to fuel financial success on the big scale and on the small scale. How do they do it? With a culture built firmly on the foundation of excellent customer service.

WHAT MAKES ACE GREAT?

In putting together this book, I interviewed scores of Ace owners, executives, and employees, also known as associates. I began each conversation with the same question: What makes Ace great?

Every single person gave me some variation on the same answer: "What makes us great is our people."

Now, I realize that that almost sounds like a cliché, that it's the kind of thing you might expect to hear from a whole lot of companies. Any company that aspires to deliver superior customer service will begin the conversation by praising its people. What makes this response from Ace a little more credible, though, is how often and how emotionally Ace's customers reach out to Ace to make exactly the same point.

Over and over again, that's what Ace's customers say: "What makes you guys great is your people." And they reach out to Ace and other people to say that without being prompted!

That state of mind and emotion—the state that turns passive customers into active evangelists—is what I call amazement.

> **AMAZEMENT:** Customer amazement starts with customer interactions that are better than average. Of course, anyone and any company can be better than average once in a while. Amazing companies, however, are better than average all of the time. It's the consistency and predictability that make these people and their companies amazing.

In this book, I'll be sharing many testimonials from amazed customers of Ace Hardware. Before I share the first of them with you, though, let me say ahead of time that I realize some of these stories are so enthusiastic that they sound like they must have been made up by the company. I promise you they are not. The only reason I have not included the last names of the individuals who shared these stories with Ace is that I did not have permission from the customers to do so. But all the testimonials are real—and all of them serve as a confirmation of Ace's long-standing brand promise: "The Helpful Place." Furthermore, that brand promise can be summed up in a single word: "Helpful."

We're going to be coming back to that word over and over again.

> "Ace store owners take pride in the time and effort
> they put into making their stores the most helpful
> hardware stores on the planet."
>
> —ACE HARDWARE

So that's the promise to the customer: to work at making Ace's stores the most helpful stores on the planet. Hyperbole? Corporate slogan-speak? Fast talk? You be the judge. Here comes the first piece of evidence.

My first example of how people are what make Ace great comes, not from Ace, but from a customer named John. I say "customer," but the truth is I'm probably jumping the gun a little bit. John was not a paying customer on the day his little adventure played out, but he wrote a fan letter anyway to his local Ace store. He had to thank them for the help he had received in dealing with a little problem he had run into—or, to be more accurate, a problem that had run into him.

John, you see, had been out riding his bike around town, and he had been hit by a car. He was injured, stunned, and still in shock when he wandered, a little dazed, into an Ace Hardware store located half a block from the scene of the accident. He asked whether the store sold bicycle wheels. (His bike's wheel, he said, had been bent so badly that it looked a little like a taco and was impossible to turn.)

Now, in case you're wondering whether Ace stores routinely stock bicycle wheels, the answer is "No." If you think that's the answer John got from the lady at the register, though, you're wrong. She said she would have to check with an associate. (Please file that little piece of information away: checking with an associate. It will become extremely important in a later chapter.)

The associate she called, whose name was Mike, apologized and told John that the store did not stock bicycle wheels, but he still wanted to help. He then followed John out of the store and took a look at the bike.

"Looking at the wheel," John later wrote in a letter, "Mike didn't seem fazed at all. 'We can fix this mountain-bike style,' he said. After we took the wheel off the bike, he proceeded to bend the damaged wheel against the curb and sidewalk, and then he used a rubber mallet to bang on the stubborn parts. Pretty soon, the wheel didn't look like a taco anymore. It looked like a normal wheel."

As John nursed his bleeding shoulder, Mike used John's spoke wrench to adjust the tension on the wheel so that it would spin properly. He pulled out some duct tape—no charge—and repaired the front fender too. In less than 15 minutes, the bike was . . . well . . . not fixed exactly, but at least in a condition that Mike could ride it home.

"Just don't hit a bump and blow the tire off," Mike warned with a smile as John drove away carefully.

Again—all this for someone who had not spent a dime in Mike's store!

Now, to the cynics who may be reading this—you know who you are—I need to acknowledge the reality that Ace "lost money" in the short term during this transaction. Yes. Duct tape costs money. Mike's time cost money. And so on. But now that I've acknowledged that, let me ask this in turn: What hardware store is John going to visit the next time he needs to buy, say, a roll of duct tape? What store is he going to recommend the next time someone mentions a home improvement, maintenance, or repair project? How many times is he going to tell friends and family members about what happened to him at Ace?

Here is what John wrote near the end of his (very long!) fan letter to Ace: "Mike, not only did you rescue a fallen cyclist and set him on his way . . . but you also restored his faith in the inherent goodness of human nature."

Wow! Now, I don't know whether or not that kind of endorsement is evidence of Ace being the most helpful hardware stores on the planet, but I do know it's evidence of being helpful. It shows that Ace is not just talking about being helpful but actually making it a reality for its customers. The difference between talking about it and actually doing it? People.

People are the key to fulfilling the brand promise. That's what Ace has figured out. And that's why you want to be Ace.

PEOPLE! POSITION! PASSION TO SERVE!

There are at least three things that make Ace great.

First, Ace's PEOPLE are the big differentiators in the marketplace. I know everybody says that, but if you spend time with Ace people, you'll recognize it and feel it for yourself. It's not just a slogan. It's actually the way they do business. What makes Ace great is people. And that starts with the people who work at the stores. Ace tells its store owners: Yes, you've got to love what you do . . . but you've got to love the who, too.

Second, Ace's POSITION makes the company great. That's because it loves being the underdog, and loves playing David and Goliath. "If you're not up on your Old Testament references, David wins that fight," Ace's CEO John Venhuizen reminded me, "so yes, we do love being in that David and Goliath position. In fact, I think what we have built our business around is the heartbeat of America: small local entrepreneurs duking it out with the big guys and winning, thanks to local customers. That's what America is all about, that's still what makes the country special. The little guy matters and can make a difference. Personally, I love coming to work with that chip on my shoulder. I love going up against some of the biggest, baddest, best-funded companies on the face of the earth."

Ace's PASSION TO SERVE is the third thing that makes it great. You want to know how Ace wins? They know that they are blessed to be in the business of serving others. That's their business. That's their place. That's the space in the industry where they dominate. And with that passion comes a special dimension of meaning and fulfillment. "You know," Venhuizen told me, "you can accomplish what looks, from a distance, like great things in this life, but if you try to make it all about you, then you do not have a fulfilled life. We know that the core of our business is that we serve others. In business, we keep score with money. We don't apologize for that or pretend it's not happening. But business isn't about money, it's about people. That's why you keep score, why you want a profitable store. We have a huge percentage of our owners who realize that being part of something bigger than themselves is really what makes life exciting."

Venhuizen went on to explain that the best Ace owners, the ones who build and support the great brand of *helpfulness* that drives the company, understand that a great, lucrative store is worth working for because it leads to four other things that are much bigger than the store.

1. **With a profitable store, owners get to better serve their own families:** If the store is doing well, the owner doesn't have to work 16-hour days, or spend too much time away from home. The first and maybe most important element of the community Ace serves is the family of the owner.

2. **With a profitable store, owners get to take great care of and serve their own people.** The associates (what many other companies call "employees") are the second tier of the community that Ace serves. When a store is not working well, when it's struggling to make ends meet, owners can't reward their people, provide health insurance, and so on. But when the store is working, they can better serve their associates, financially and in other ways. People sometimes forget that one of the really important ways a company serves the community is by meeting its payroll!

3. **With a profitable store, owners get to better serve their customers and the larger community.** When you have a store that's very

profitable, you can better serve the larger community, including customers and future customers—like the gentleman on the bike. When you can give that kind of service to the community, some really special things start to happen in the marketplace.

4. **With a profitable store, owners get to better serve the least, the littlest, and the lonely.** Once you are running a profitable store, you don't have to make every single decision according to what makes the most sense for the bottom line. You can give something back financially. For a whole lot of Ace owners, what they do to help others in need is what they're proudest of achieving. That's moving from success to significance. That's the highest point on the human development pyramid.

But *without* a successful, profitable store, the owner would never get to serve these four critical parts of the community. That's *why* Ace keeps score. That's why they compete on amazement. And that's why they win.

From a distance, all this can sound a little "out there," but internally it's what sustains the company and makes it special from the inside out. Ace owners believe in this culture. And they live this culture. You can believe in, and live, a culture like that too.

Now, how could you not want to be part of a company that operates like that? How could you not want your company to embody the idea that people really are what makes the difference?

This book will show you how.

It will show you how to create and sustain an amazement culture based on people—both employees and customers.

It will show you how you can help to create and support this culture, and to deliver the kind of amazing service that wins evangelists, regardless of whether you:

- Own and operate a small business (including a one-person business)

- Are responsible for managing a larger business

- Are part of a larger business but do not have managerial responsibility

Most important of all, you'll learn how to *live*—not just talk about—a workplace culture rooted in the concept of Amazing Every Customer Every Time!

YOUR AMAZEMENT TOOLBOX

- Amazement is the state of mind and emotion that turns passive customers into customer evangelists.

- Customer amazement starts with customer interactions that are better than average.

- Any company can be better than average once in a while. *Amazing* companies are better than average all of the time.

- The Ace Hardware mantra is just one word: "Helpful." They take pride in being the most *helpful* hardware stores on the planet.

- The difference between just talking about customer service and delivering amazement lies in people.

- People are the key to fulfilling a company's brand promise.

- John Venhuizen, Ace CEO, says, "We are blessed to be in the business of serving others."

- A culture of helpful sustains Ace and makes it special from the inside out. Ace owners believe in this culture.

- A profitable business allows you the luxury of serving your family, employees, community, and people in need.

CHAPTER FOUR

OPERATIONALIZING HELPFUL

An amazing customer service culture begins by first amazing the employees.

HOW DO YOU TURN a good idea for a culture into reality? By building an employee-centered workplace.

How do you make an amazing culture happen where it hasn't happened before? How do you *operationalize* that culture? How do you move beyond posters and slogans that people tune out (or, even worse, ridicule)? How do you create a day-by-day reality where people actually respond with the focused attention and concern that customers remember, appreciate, and can't help talking about to family and friends? How do you change what actually happens to the customer?

Ace has figured out the answer: By first changing what happens to the people who work in the store.

Ace Hardware has figured out that in order to build a customer-centric business you must first build an *employee-centric business.* This is one of the great central principles embraced by enterprises that consistently deliver amazing customer service. They know that amazement starts at home.

In part two of this book, I'll be sharing lots of strategies and tools you can use at all levels of your organization to deliver an amazing customer experience. But what you have to understand before you start looking at any of those resources is that none of those tools are likely to work for your organization unless employees experience the amazement for themselves first.

That's how you truly instill a great service culture: by making sure the employees actually experience what you are asking them to deliver to the customer.

Think about it. If your car's front end is out of alignment, then the entire car is going to shake. It's not so different in business. If the front line doesn't experience the same value promise that is supposed to be delivered to the customer, then the entire company can suffer.

This employee-centered philosophy of Ace reminds me of exactly how Herb Kelleher, cofounder, Chairman Emeritus, and former CEO of Southwest Airlines, ran his very successful airline. Kelleher recognized that you have to put your employees first. If you do, they will treat the customers (in his case, the passengers) well. Then, the passengers will come back and fly on the airline again. And that, by the way, will also make the shareholders very happy.

Operationalizing a good service culture just means putting your employees first. Nothing more, nothing less. So if you want your customers to experience helpful, you have to make sure your company's employees are operating in an environment where helpful is actually how people interact with one another!

This is why one of the crucial phases that any company has to go through to create high levels of service is alignment.

Alignment is the process by which everyone in the company experiences the vision firsthand. Everyone must be pointed in the same direction—toward the brand promise. It starts with the right people who have the right mindset.

One of the ways Ace ensures alignment with its culture is through extensive training that "certifies" both the store and the associates. In a new training initiative centered solely on the customer experience, Ace wants every associate in every store to go through Helpful 101 certification on their way to becoming Certified Ace Helpful. This is not product training. This is focused exclusively on getting all associates into alignment, thereby fulfilling the *helpful* brand promise.

Furthermore, just getting the Helpful 101 certification isn't enough. Each store must requalify annually and be willing to be surveyed and mystery-shopped monthly. In other words, they must sustain helpful. If there is a decrease in their Helpful Index, Ace corporate will help the stores determine how and why the scores dropped, and help them to recover.

Everybody gets the mission as something that directly affects them, personally, in a powerful, positive way. Everybody buys into the mission not because of a poster on the wall that nobody actually lives by but because, along with the training, *they personally experience the very best expression of that mission, firsthand, on a day-to-day basis.*

In addition to training, another absolutely indispensable cultural tool for creating this level of alignment is something I call the company mantra.

This mantra is a key phrase that is extremely short, yet so simple that when employees and customers hear it, they know exactly what the company is all about. They know what is driving the behavior, the decisions, and the problem solving, both within the company and in its interactions with external customers. (Note: Some amazing companies create separate mantras for internal and external customers, which is fine.)

These are key phrases that make it crystal clear, for both the employees and their customers, what the company is trying to achieve, both internally and externally.

One of my favorite examples of a mantra that drives internal and external experiences comes from Horst Schulze, former president of the Ritz-Carlton Hotels. At age 15, he wrote a term paper, the title of which Ritz-Carlton Hotels adopted as its motto (and now preaches to its employees and demonstrates to its guests): "We are ladies and gentlemen serving ladies and gentlemen." I've mentioned this in previous books and articles because it's such a great example. That one phrase instantly tells you everything you need to know about what standards drive interactions among employees inside that company—and interactions between employees and customers. If you've ever stayed at one of the hotels, you know that the Ritz-Carlton is usually in full *alignment* with this mantra.

Another great mantra is that of the online retail giant Zappos.com. What is that organization all about? "Delivering happiness." Considering how often that company has shown up on prominent lists of the best places to work in America, and the high customer satisfaction ratings it routinely scores, it's a sure bet that its mantra is something Zappos.com's employees buy into.

And by this point, I hope you can guess what Ace's mantra is. It's one I really love, because its most commonly expressed version is exactly one word long: "Helpful." The longer version, as previously mentioned, is still short; just three words: "The Helpful Place." But, for the purpose of this book, I want you to keep your eye on how well Ace operationalizes that one word—"helpful"—for its own people before it expects them to deliver helpful to their own customers.

In this book, we will be looking at many different ways Ace makes absolutely sure its owners and associates are in full alignment with this powerful and easy-to-remember mantra. In fact, I consider it to be the gold standard when it comes to effective mantras for service-driven companies! Ace has grasped that you can't operationalize a culture that people don't remember, can't understand, or haven't experienced directly.

MAKING HELPFUL A DAILY REALITY

Ace Hardware's corporate headquarters provides many superb resources and tools to help an Ace owner deliver helpful. But, you are not limited to just what headquarters provides. As an owner, you are free to come up with your own methods of doing business, especially if it promotes the concept of helpful.

So, imagine that you own an Ace Hardware store. And imagine that you come up with a specific tool to help you create and deliver helpful. By the way, the tool I'm referring to is not a hammer or a saw. This is a business tool, and it is designed to help you build better relationships with your customers by building better relationships with your employees. This particular resource that you really like is an internal initiative known as the Five-Dollar Lifeboat.

What is the Five-Dollar Lifeboat? Basically, it's an internal spending policy, one that you, as an Ace owner, can choose to adopt, or not, as you see fit. This policy empowers any associate at your store to spend up to five dollars on his or her own initiative, without prior approval, on any customer, at any time, and on as many individual customer problems as necessary, to solve an individual customer's problem . . . and make him or her smile. Whatever form the lifeboat may need to take, if it costs five dollars or less, the associate can toss it into the water, solve the problem, and get the customer back on dry land.

Great idea, right? If it's possible to solve the problem for less than five dollars, why wouldn't you want to empower your people to do so? Why would you want your people to even *think* about arguing with a customer over a five-dollar solution to a problem? And notice that the first message you're sending here is not to the customer but to the Ace associate. That message to that associate is both simple and powerful: "I trust you. Do what you think is right in these situations." That's one of the critical lessons Ace has learned over the years, by the way: Good culture starts with the employees, not the customers. You may notice that I come back to that theme again and again in this book. It's that important.

So here's my question to you: Once you decide that that initiative is right for your store, how would you launch it?

Would you put up a poster? Would you send out a mass email and remind everyone to read it? Would you alter the policy manual and send everyone a copy of the new document?

No, no, and no. If you were one of the successful Ace stores driven by an amazement-savvy entrepreneur, you would *amaze* your associates by telling, and constantly retelling, this true story.

Let me tell you about one of the Ace owners from a few decades back, a wonderful guy named Elder Glenn. He owned a store in Chattanooga, Tennessee. One day he saw a customer walk into his store with an agitated look on his face. The customer, whose name was Bill, made his way up to the counter, introduced himself, and said to Elder, "I've got a problem."

"What's that?" Elder asked.

Bill explained that he had bought two products at this particular Ace store, each with the offer of a five-dollar rebate. Bill said he had completed all the paperwork properly and mailed it to the manufacturer. Weeks and weeks had gone by, but he hadn't received his rebate checks. And he was tired of waiting.

Elder realized that his customer was pretty worked up about this rebate issue. So he turned to the cashier who was standing next to him and said, "Lisa, why don't you open the register and hand me two five-dollar bills."

Lisa did exactly that, and Elder handed Bill the money and said, "Go ahead and take this. If the rebate check comes in, and you want to swing by the store and give us back the ten dollars, that would be fine."

The customer was pleasantly surprised, took the money, and thanked Elder.

From that moment on, Elder had a customer for life. Not only that—he had a friend for life. Every time Bill came into the store, he made a point of finding Elder and saying hello.

That's the kind of result you're going to have with your customers using Elder's new policy called the Five-Dollar Lifeboat.

Look at the four *amazing* things that this true story accomplishes:

1. It shows what the mantra—helpful—looks like in action.
2. It tells the associate, "We trust you to do this, and we trust you to do it right." Trust is a key part of building an employee-centric organization, which is something we'll be talking about in more detail in part two of this book.
3. It tells the customer, "We trust you." That's huge, and it's another point we will be coming back to later on.
4. It immediately conveys both the letter and the spirit of the policy, and it does so in a way that is easy for associates to remember and repeat.

How much is a lifetime customer worth to you? What would you pay? Five dollars? Five hundred dollars? Other organizations have similar policies. The Ritz-Carlton hotel chain empowers its employees to spend up to two thousand dollars to take care of a guest's problem.

Obviously, there has to be some training and guidelines shared to make this a successful strategy, be it a five-dollar strategy or a two-thousand-dollar strategy. In just a moment, you'll see how this story comes to life, as it moves from taking care of an upset customer to helping a customer in need.

> HELPFUL is Ace's culture in a word—its mantra. It's essential to have a brief phrase that exemplifies where you're going as an organization.

Not long after he had heard the Five-Dollar Lifeboat story as part of his training, a newly hired associate at that same Ace Hardware store made a key for one of his customers—and then ran into a problem.

The customer realized *after* the key had been made for her that she had forgotten her purse. She couldn't pay. She asked the young man if he would mind holding on to the key for her while she went home and got her purse.

The helpful teenager said, "Don't worry, ma'am. I'll pay for it myself. It's not that much. When you remember, just come on back to the store and we can settle up. Here's your key. Thank you for your business."

She took the key and thanked him, but before she made it out of the store, a funny feeling came over her. Was she doing the right thing? Quietly, she sought out a manager and explained what had happened. She told the manager that she definitely did not want to get the nice young man in trouble, but she also didn't want to leave the store without making sure the manager approved of what he had done.

The manager laughed and assured her that the young clerk had done exactly as he had been trained to do. "The only mistake he made," he assured her, "was paying for the key himself. The company will pay him back. I'll let him know, and you can rest assured that he's not in any trouble at all. Exactly the opposite, he will be commended."

She left, smiling . . . and *amazed*. Another friendship—and another customer for life!

That's what *helpful* looks like in action. When it's operationalized successfully, it feels good to the customer and feels good to the associate who provides the service. It also delivers on the mantra, which is also the Ace brand promise: to be *helpful*—specifically, to be the most helpful hardware stores on the planet.

YOUR AMAZEMENT TOOLBOX

- To change to a customer-focused culture, start by changing what happens to the employees.

- To deliver customer amazement, employees must first experience amazement for themselves.

- Employees must be in alignment with amazement. If a car's front end is out of alignment, the car shakes. It's the same in business.

- Alignment is the process by which every employee experiences and understands the company's vision and mission.

- Training helps teach the vision and mission, but employees must put the training into action for it to have any meaning.

- A mantra (in business) simplifies the company's vision and mission into a short phrase that everyone understands.

- Sharing true stories about customer-focused policies like the Five-Dollar Lifeboat empowers employees.

CHAPTER FIVE

THE SEVEN AMAZEMENT PRINCIPLES

Moments of Magic are what make amazement possible.

THERE ARE SEVEN KEY principles that you will need to understand in order to use the 52 Amazement Tools to their full effectiveness. Let's look at each of them now.

PRINCIPLE #1: THE MOMENT OF MAGIC

Have you ever gotten service that was so outstanding that you promised yourself you'd go back and buy from the same place so you could enjoy the experience all over again?

Maybe you were in a restaurant, and you found the service and food so outstanding that you left an extra-large tip. Or maybe you were in a hotel where all the staff seemed courteous and helpful, and truly made you feel like a VIP. Or maybe, just maybe, you went to a local hardware store, perhaps without even realizing what the name of the store was, and suddenly found yourself treated like a member of the family. (By now, I'll bet you can guess what the name of that hardware store probably is, but I digress.)

All of these are examples of what I call Moments of Magic. I'm sure you have some examples of your own that mean more to you than the ones I just shared, experiences of above-average service that stand out in your memory just because, before you had your Moment of Magic, you were so used to receiving average or below-average service. A Moment of Magic entails getting something a little better or a little more than you expected. Sometimes it's something that's delivered with a distinctly personal touch. It's proof that someone cared enough to see that your experience was superior. That's within the reach of everyone.

Once you have been treated to a moment like this, you feel extra satisfaction, knowing that someone (or a company) has gone the extra mile to serve you. No matter what business or occupation you are in, you can use the Moments of Magic concept to achieve greater success. When you consistently create Moments of Magic, your customers will want to do business with you again and again—and will tell all their friends to do business with you. Without Moments of Magic, you cannot possibly amaze your customers!

And by the way, when I say "customers," please assume that I am using a catchall phrase that also describes patients, guests, subscribers, passengers, and any other label you may choose to apply to those people you want to amaze on a regular basis.

Now, I've mentioned that creating Moments of Magic is about going above and beyond or going the extra mile. There is an important qualifier here, though. Don't think that a Moment of Magic always has to be a WOW experience or something that is truly "over-the-top." It's actually much easier than that. A Moment of Magic, at a minimum, just has to simply be above average. So at the very least, a Moment of Magic is just a little above average, and at its best it really is a WOW experience. Either way, it's what it takes to create amazement!

PRINCIPLE #2: THE MOMENT OF TRUTH

Now we know: A Moment of Magic is what happens when you receive above-average service. A Moment of Truth is the opportunity to make that

Moment of Magic happen—an opportunity that some companies take full advantage of, and other companies don't.

Each and every interaction we have with a customer, be it person-to-person or online, is a Moment of Truth. At that moment, we have the chance to leave a positive or a negative feeling with the customer about the experience. That feeling we leave with the customer can make or break our business.

I didn't come up with this concept of the Moment of Truth. That honor goes to Jan Carlzon, the author of the book *Moments of Truth* (Ballinger, 1987), who was the former president of Scandinavian Airlines, better known as SAS. Carlzon defined the Moment of Truth like this:

> **Any time a customer comes into contact with any aspect of your business, however remote, they have an opportunity to form an impression.**

Carlzon identified a number of particularly critical Moments of Truth for his airline. These included:

- When passengers make reservations;

- At the curb when they check their bags;

- At the ticket counter when they purchase or confirm their tickets;

- When they are greeted as they board the plane;

- When they are greeted at their destination; and

- At the baggage claim area when they pick up their bags.

Of course, there are many other Moments of Truth that can happen in between these experiences. A passenger might be walking down the concourse toward the gate and might pass an employee of the airline. If that employee smiles, that might be a positive Moment of Truth. It's not a main Moment of Truth, but it is still a very important one. Remember

that every Moment of Truth, even the smallest interaction, is an opportunity for a customer to form an opinion or impression of the company.

PRINCIPLE #3: THE MOMENT OF MISERY

A Moment of Misery is what happens when a Moment of Truth is mishandled. Unfortunately, this is an all too common experience. If you've
ever found yourself waiting too long for the server at the restaurant to
notice you, or gotten an alarmingly large bill you couldn't make sense of
from an auto repair shop, you've experienced a Moment of Misery. Notice
again that it doesn't have to be extreme. This can be a major complaint or
problem or just a below-average experience.

Any Moment of Truth can go well—or go poorly. Even great service
companies have their share of Moments of Misery. No one person, no
company, is perfect. And the great companies recognize this, but they also
know that Moments of Misery can be turned into Moments of Magic.
They have trained their people and have systems in place to deal with
complaints and problems. It is all in the "recovery."

Our job is to take any Moment of Misery, seize it as an opportunity to
create a Moment of Magic, and show how good we are!

PRINCIPLE #4: THE MOMENT OF MEDIOCRITY

According to Jan Carlzon, the Moment of Truth can go two ways: good
or bad. Now you know that I refer to them as Moments of Magic or
Moments of Misery. But there is a third possibility Carlzon didn't talk
about. That is the Moment of Mediocrity.

A Moment of Truth that is just average is a Moment of Mediocrity. It's
neither bad nor good. It's just okay. Satisfactory. Nothing special.

Imagine you are walking into a restaurant at the very same moment
that I'm walking out. You ask me, "Shep, how's the food?" I tell you that
it's okay, nothing special. In other words, not particularly bad or good, just
satisfactory. Are you going to be excited about spending your hard-earned

money at a restaurant that is just "okay"? If you do decide to eat there (maybe you're short on time), are you going to go out of your way to tell other people about it? Probably not.

That average, nothing-special Moment of Mediocrity is what too many companies deliver. Even if the customer comes back, at any given time the customer may realize that there is a better place to do business, and most likely will quietly switch to a competitor.

PRINCIPLE #5: CUSTOMER AMAZEMENT

This is what this book is all about: Amazing Every Customer Every Time! That's a lofty goal—but a very achievable goal.

It starts with managing the Moment of Truth and creating Moments of Magic. That means that you have a goal that each and every interaction you have with the customer has to be better than average. Just a little better than average!

It may be as simple as the way you smile and greet someone when they walk through your doors or into your office. Or it may be the amazing experience you create when you really do go above and beyond what is expected. The goal is that every seemingly insignificant interaction, as well as the biggest experience, needs to be better than average.

Amazing companies don't just deliver Moments of Magic. They *consistently* and *predictably* deliver Moments of Magic. While it is easy for anyone or any company to be above average some of the time, it is the great ones that are above average all of the time. And that is what amazement is: consistently and predictably better than average.

PRINCIPLE #6: INTERNAL AND EXTERNAL CUSTOMERS

"I don't deal directly with the public, so my job doesn't involve customer service."

Wrong!

To understand why this is so, you must understand that there are really two types of customers: internal and external. The external customer is the buyer of your company's product or service. You also have many internal customers. These are the people who don't interact directly with the customer but who do affect the external customer experience. In the final analysis, of course, everything everyone in your company does affects the external customer experience. We have to amaze our internal customers if we want our external customers to be amazed!

In their great book *Service America* (Grand Central Publishing, 1990), Ron Zemke and Karl Albrecht write, "If you're not serving the customer, you'd better be serving someone who is." Truer words were never written!

Some companies—Ace is one of them—have learned one of the central lessons of delivering truly amazing customer service: In order for external customers to experience amazing service consistently, internal customers must first experience amazing internal service consistently.

You may be familiar with the term "customer-centric." This describes a company that operates on the principle that everyone who works for the company, and every responsibility assigned within it, should put the customer first. Everyone, everywhere, should put the customer at the "top-of-mind" level. How does a company become customer-centric? By recognizing the importance of internal service. I call such companies "employee-centric." They have figured out that there must be internal amazement before there can be external amazement.

PRINCIPLE #7: THE FIVE STAGES

As we have just seen, some companies choose to amaze their customers first. There are some companies that create a powerful "brand promise" (what I refer to as a "mantra") that works internally/externally. If you want your company to Amaze Every Customer Every Time, you want to be this kind of company. That means everyone in the company must move through five distinct stages (referred to as "Cults" in the book *The Cult of the Customer* [Wiley, 2009]) in relation to that brand promise on their way to experiencing amazement. Those stages are:

1. Uncertainty: The employee, also known as the internal customer, is not yet aware or convinced that the brand promise even exists or can be fulfilled.

2. Alignment: The employee understands what the brand promise is.

3. Experience: The employee experiences the brand promise and likes the results.

4. Ownership: The employee experiences the brand promise enough to be confident that it will happen the next time—and every time.

5. Amazement: The experience that the employee owns is consistently above average. As a result, he or she becomes an advocate and evangelist for promoting and fulfilling the brand promise.

Just as the employees go through these stages, customers go through the exact same ones. The first time customers do business with an organization they are uncertain, but hoping, that it will be a good experience. They may understand the brand promise, which means they are in alignment with the company, but they haven't yet experienced it. Once they have experienced the promise, and they are confident it will happen again, they have ownership of the brand promise. And, if that experience is consistently better than average, they have been treated to customer amazement.

Only when an internal customer has gone through these five stages can he or she be expected to lead a customer through them!

It might not seem obvious at first, but once you think about it, you realize that truly great service companies are always employee-centric before they are customer-centric. One of the most important lessons you will learn in this book is that, in order to create a customer-centric company, you must first create an employee-centric company. What's happening on the inside of an organization is always being felt on the outside by its customers.

Ace Hardware has built an employee-centric company. Does being an employee-centric company mean Ace is perfect? Of course not. But it's got a mantra that everyone agrees on, inside and out. By now you know that its promise, its mantra, can be summed up in a single word: "Helpful." It's because Ace lives that mantra internally that it can deliver on the promise externally.

YOU ARE READY TO ROLL!

Congratulations! You now have the background you need to put the tools in the following chapters into practice. Let's get started!

YOUR AMAZEMENT TOOLBOX

- A Moment of Magic is when you receive above-average service.

- A Moment of Truth is any time a customer has an opportunity to form an impression.

- A Moment of Misery is what happens when a Moment of Truth is mishandled.

- Moments of Misery can be turned into Moments of Magic with a good recovery.

- In order for external customers to experience amazement (consistent Moments of Magic), internal customers must experience it first.

- There are five steps to great service: uncertainty, alignment, experience, ownership, and amazement.

- Employees must go through the five stages leading to customer amazement before they can be expected to lead customers through them!

- Whatever is happening on the inside of an organization is being felt on the outside by the customers.

PART TWO

THE 52 TOOLS FOR CUSTOMER AMAZEMENT

"People who lead—whether or not they have a title—strive to make things better for those around them. They increase what I call ROI. In this instance ROI doesn't stand for 'return on investment,' but rather Relationships, Outcomes and Improvements."

—MARK SANBORN

WHEN IT COMES TO customer service, it all starts with leadership. And believe it or not, everyone can, and should, assume a leadership role when it comes to building a culture of service. Leaders know how to deal with customers one-on-one and will take advantage of numerous competitive edges to differentiate their enterprise from the competition. Finally, leaders understand that it's all about the relationship with their customers and willingly give back to their community because they value the loyalty the community has shown them.

These five elements—leadership, culture, one-on-one interaction, a desire to create and sustain a competitive edge, and a willingness to contribute to the community—are the recipe for success. You will find that recipe in the pages that follow.

CHAPTER SIX

LEADERSHIP

"Leadership is not about titles, positions, or flowcharts. It is about one life influencing another."

—JOHN C. MAXWELL

DON'T GET HUNG UP on the word "leadership." When it comes to amazing your customers, everyone, regardless of title or responsibility, can be a leader—and that includes you, whatever your job title. The most amazing companies, in fact, are those in which everyone assumes a leadership role.

You really do have the opportunity to be a great role model for the customer, as well as for all the people with whom you work, in delivering an amazing service experience. What you will find in this chapter of the book are nine Amazement Tools that can make it easy for you to deliver that great example.

Leadership Tools

1. Act Like You Own the Place

2. Trust

3. Debrief on Both Misery and Magic

4. Befriend the Competition

5. Adapt or Die

6. Know the Value of Your Customers

7. Know What Drives Your Success

8. You Can't Be Good at Everything

9. Play to Your Strengths

1

ACT LIKE
YOU OWN THE PLACE

*Take so much pride in what you do that your customers think you
are the owner.*

AFTER A RECENT PRESENTATION on customer service I gave in Colorado, a young man named Clark, who worked at a pizza restaurant, came up to me and shared something with me that made me feel very proud to do what I do for a living. He looked me in the eye and said, "Shep, I want to be so good that my customers ask me if I am the owner!"

Wow! I hope he mentioned that aspiration to his boss, the owner of the pizza restaurant. If he did, I know that's at least two people who feel proud of their line of work—me and the owner of that pizza restaurant!

If Clark follows through on that goal—and I have to believe he does, every day—his boss will pick up on Clark's positive attitude, on the excellent service he delivers, on the way he treats fellow employees, and a lot more.

Obviously, Clark respects and admires the owner. And obviously, the owner of the restaurant has set a good example, one that Clark wants to emulate. That's incredibly important, because *amazement starts at the top.* An owner must be a good role model, a good mentor, and a good leader, and so must anyone else in a position of leadership. If you're privileged to lead your team, make sure that everyone who reports to you would want to emulate your actions and decisions! I've seen plenty of owners/leaders who don't set good examples with their "do as I say, not as I do" management style. That's a shame.

Typically, that's not what you find at Ace Hardware. I interviewed dozens of owners for this book, and dozens of associates too. What I found, in every single case, was an owner who "walks the walk." By that I mean an owner whose example is worth following, someone the associates want to emulate. Every single owner I spoke to or watched in action came across as someone who was friendly and accessible to employees, who embodied integrity, who was flexible in addressing challenges when they arose, and who was *helpful*, first and foremost. Guess what! That's exactly the way Ace associates treat their customers!

If you are the owner, your job is to be so great at what you do that employees aspire to be just like you. If you are the employee, your job is to be so great at what you do that customers mistake you for the owner!

Regardless of the size of your company, regardless of who you are or what you do, act like an owner!

YOUR AMAZEMENT TOOLBOX

- An owner (or manager) must be a good role model, a good mentor, and a good leader.

- If you're a leader, make sure everyone who reports to you would want to emulate your actions and decisions.

- Regardless of the size of your company, regardless of your job title, and regardless of what you do, act like an owner!

THE DRILL

- Who are the leaders in your company (whether or not they have the title)?

- If you are the owner or manager, what can you do to develop leaders in your organization?

- If you are an employee, do you take as much pride and "ownership" in your responsibilities as the owner or CEO? If so, share an example.

2

TRUST

A little well-earned trust in employees and colleagues goes a long way in improving the customer experience.

BACK WHEN I WAS 21 YEARS OLD, I got myself a job working at Central City Auto Parts in St. Louis, Missouri. The owner and my boss, Barry Wolkowitz, must have liked my style, because he left me in charge of the place for a couple of days while he went off on the first vacation he had taken in years. I had only been working there for about two months, but there I was, getting ready to manage the entire business in his absence!

The very first day I was running the store on my own, I had to make a judgment call. A customer brought up a big plastic container of antifreeze, and the darned thing didn't have a price tag on it. I suppose I'm dating myself by admitting this now, but this was back in the days before we could swipe barcodes over automatic readers or punch codes into an inventory system whenever a price tag was missing. Back then you had to manually look up the price in a large bank of merchandise catalogs, and as hard as I looked, I couldn't track down the price for this antifreeze. So I guessed. I told the customer, "Look, I can't find the price for this thing. Let's just say it's five dollars."

The customer looked at me, nodded, said, "You've got a deal," turned around, went back into the aisle where he'd found the original container, and came back with *three cases* of antifreeze.

He looked me in the eye and said, "Five bucks, right?"

What could I do? I'd made a deal. I sold him three cases of antifreeze at five bucks a pop.

When Barry came back, I told him exactly what had happened, and he was completely understanding about my mistake. He said, "Hey, you made a bad call, it happens. Don't worry about it." Then he showed me where I was supposed to have found the right price, which was in a whole different book. It turned out I was supposed to have charged *twelve bucks a gallon*. Oops! Although my boss wanted to be sure I didn't make the same mistake all over again, he also wanted me to know that he knew that mistakes were part of the learning process. So he didn't start yelling and screaming at me over my mistake. To the contrary, he said, "At the end of the day, Shep, I can't be looking over your shoulder on every decision you make with a customer. I know you're going to make a lot more good calls than bad calls."

Here's the point: He still trusted me, even though I had messed up. And the moment I realized that, I knew that I was very lucky indeed to work there. Because this man still trusted me, I was even more motivated than before to prove that I deserved that trust. And I think I did a better job of serving the customers, giving them advice that they could trust, as a result of that experience.

Regarding that same point, Ace's CEO John Venhuizen told me, "Every time a customer walks through our doors, that customer is trusting our associates to help them to solve a problem, and to buy the right product. Possibly, that solution we come up with involves the home where their kids sleep every night. Now, whenever you accept advice from someone about what you're supposed to do in order to protect and take care of your home, that's a significant leap of faith. That means the level of trust and emotional connection that associate needs to be able to build up with the customer is huge. By the same token, the trust and emotional connection the store owner builds up with the associate has to be pretty huge too. So we know that, in order to win that high level of trust with the consumer, we have to establish a trusting relationship with the employee first."

YOUR AMAZEMENT TOOLBOX

- Empower your employees to make decisions on their own, even if it means making a mistake.

- Once an employee has earned your trust, make sure the employee knows it.

- Mistakes happen. The question is whether the employee learned enough from the mistake to keep it from happening again.

- The level of trust you establish with your employees affects the level of trust your employees establish with customers.

THE DRILL

- When was the last time a manager or a colleague entrusted you with an important responsibility, and how did it make you feel?

- If you are a manager, what steps can you take to empower your employees, and how do you handle the situation when an employee makes a mistake?

3

DEBRIEF ON BOTH MISERY AND MAGIC

Don't just figure out how to keep Moments of Misery from happening again . . . figure out how to reproduce Moments of Magic.

IF I HAD TO PICK a single, easy-to-follow best practice that sets Ace apart from other service companies, it would be this one. I saw and heard evidence of it over and over again, at every store I visited and in every interview with every successful Ace owner I talked to. This best practice boils down to six simple words: *Misery leaves clues. Magic leaves clues.*

Some companies are already pretty good at the first half of this. When a customer makes a complaint about a Moment of Misery that he or she experienced, management will take a good, long look at that complaint. Sometimes, management will figure out that the problem was an employee who gave a customer a bad attitude. But sometimes, they'll figure out that there was a problem of some kind in the system. Something fell through the cracks, and might fall through the cracks again. Management concludes that the company needs to change the way it does things. In that scenario, management will have a debrief meeting, either formal or informal, and figure out exactly what steps need to be taken to keep that particular Moment of Misery from happening again. That debrief meeting spots all the clues that point toward the true causes of the Moment of Misery, and it allows management to change whatever needs to be changed to reduce the impact of the problem or even eliminate the possibility of it happening in the future.

Where Ace goes a little further than most companies is in the second half of the equation. Ace knows that a Moment of Magic leaves clues too! Whenever a fan letter, meaning a letter from a recently amazed customer, comes in, they don't just congratulate the associate, stick a copy in the person's file, and move on. They also hold a debrief session, just like the one where they tried to figure out what caused the Moment of Misery. Only this time, they are looking for clues to the Moment of Magic that caused the customer to want to write the accolade letter. What made it possible? What could make it easier to reproduce? What could make this kind of experience happen for every customer every time?

Ace is one of those great companies that's committed to learn all it can from its happiest customers. You can be part of that kind of company too. Whatever role you play in your organization, you can try to engage, in greater depth, with your happiest customers. Talk to them to learn about the details that made this particular interaction successful. Go back to the team and analyze why things worked. Is what happened to this customer the norm? If not, could it be? Can it be improved upon? Can it be repeated? Why did this interaction stand out to this customer while others didn't? Do other customers have similar ecstatically happy experiences?

We can learn as much from our successes as we can from our failures—if not more. Don't just revel in success. Learn from it!

YOUR AMAZEMENT TOOLBOX

- Moments of Misery leave clues. Moments of Magic leave clues. Look for the root causes of both experiences, and learn!

- Learn from your happy customers, especially if they are willing to tell you their story, so you can repeat it with others.

- We can learn as much from our Moments of Magic as we can from our Moments of Misery—if not more.

THE DRILL

- What is the most important lesson you have learned from a happy customer?

- What is the most important lesson you have learned from an unhappy customer?

4

BEFRIEND THE COMPETITION

Keep your friends close and your enemies closer.

THIS FAMOUS PIECE OF ADVICE is commonly attributed to Michael Corleone in *The Godfather, Part II*, and is an excellent business strategy, even if the original quote comes from Niccolò Machiavelli, who wrote *The Prince*.

Whoever said it, the point is that you can learn a lot from your competition. And you should! Too many companies make the mistake of turning their competitors into "bad guys." They get into the habit of assuming that everything the competition does is driven by some kind of bad intent. Sure, they want to be successful, and that may mean taking some of your customers and stealing away market share. However, the problem with persistently labeling your competition as the villain is that once you do, it becomes harder to pick up information you need about them that will help you compete.

Keeping a sense of perspective and an open mind about what the competition is doing can help you be a much more effective competitor in the marketplace. In my business of speaking, training, and consulting on customer service, there are many prominent and worthy competitors.

Do I try to avoid them? No. Do I see them as my enemy? No. On the contrary, I see them on a regular basis at conventions. I call them to meet for dinner if I'm in their city. I exchange ideas on how to be more success- ful in the business. We may be competitors, but we recognize and believe what Cavett Robert, the founder of the National Speakers Association, once said:

Don't worry about how we divide up the pie; there is enough for everybody. Let's just build a bigger pie!

One way or another, our competition is going to get their slice of the pie. So what can we do to keep them from making our slice smaller—or worse, making it disappear?

Everyone deserves a slice of the pie. Why not make the pie bigger? Sean Curry, an Ace Hardware store owner in Boston, recognizes the value of the fact that he can't avoid competition. He can walk out of his store and look either direction and see the competition—a big-box home improvement store to his right, and another big-box home improvement store to his left! Some people might think that two major competitors could put Sean's store out of business. After all, they are huge compared to Sean's small store. They outspend Sean in advertising by 20 to 30 times.

So, what did Sean do? He asked the other stores' managers out to lunch. He wanted to introduce himself, welcome them to the neighbor- hood, and talk about how they could work together.

He wanted to find out what he could stock that they didn't, and vice versa. He offered to send customers to their stores, if appropriate. They offered to do the same!

The concept of building a friendly relationship with your competitors is a sound one. Sean gets customer referrals from both stores. He knows their shortcomings, and he recognizes how he can capitalize on them. He knows his strengths and makes sure he can exploit them. By keeping the lines of communication open, he not only competes with but also flour- ishes next to these much larger competitors.

The more information you have about what the other guys are doing, the better the job you can do for your own customers. Not only that, understanding what the other guys do well in the marketplace is essential if you want to continue improving on what *you* do well in the marketplace. (See Tool #8: You Can't Be Good at Everything.)

John Venhuizen, Ace's CEO, told me: "We never put down the 'big box' players in our industry. They are great retailers, and we are the first to acknowledge that. We also know, though, that one of the things that makes them great is their bigness. They're huge. Because they are huge, the service and the convenience tend to be weaknesses in the experience they offer to the consumer. Knowing their strengths and weaknesses in the marketplace reminds us where we can be strong. We're smaller, we're speedier, we're a more integral part of the community, and of course we're more helpful. Every time we look at a 'big box' store, we get a reminder that we're local and loyal, which is right where we want to be and where we ought to be."

YOUR AMAZEMENT TOOLBOX

- Don't demonize your competition. Learn what they do best. Knowing about your competition can make you a better competitor.

- Know your competition's shortcomings and capitalize on them. Know your strengths and exploit them.

- Consider taking the competition out to lunch.

- Use what you know about your competition to differentiate the experience you deliver to the consumer in the marketplace.

- Let your research on what the competition does best remind you of what you do best.

THE DRILL

- How do your company's strengths differ from those of your competitors? Do these strengths give you an advantage that generates referrals from competitors?

- For managers: How much do you know about your direct competition? How could you find out more?

5

ADAPT OR DIE

Listen to your customers . . . and learn what changes they expect.

WHAT WOULD YOU THINK of a supermarket that refused to take a debit card . . . because there had been no such thing as a debit card when the store was founded, 50 years ago? "Cash only, please!"

What would you think of a consultant who chooses not to communicate with his clients via email . . . because email didn't exist when he graduated from college back in the '80s? "Hey, watch your postal deliveries carefully over the next few days; I just sent you a detailed report, via First Class Mail, about that time-sensitive business problem that you paid me to look at. Drop me a postcard once you've had the chance to look it over. I'll write you back, and then we can schedule a meeting."

What would you think of a start-up business that wants to build up a national following rapidly . . . without setting up a website or any kind of social media presence? "Internet, schminternet. My dad launched his business without any of this online stuff, and I don't need anything like that for my business, either. If people want to find out about us, they can call our toll-free line or look at the brochures we're printing."

I know what I'd think about each of these businesses. I'd be wondering how closely they'd really been listening to their customers. And I'd also wonder how much longer they could expect to stay in business—if they didn't adapt.

You might laugh at these examples, but the truth is, for some it can be very hard to admit that times have changed, and that our responsibilities to the customer have changed too. That's especially true when we've grown used to doing things a certain way. Sometimes, we build up a preconceived notion of how something should work. We may think, "Hey, we've always done it that way. Why fix something that isn't broken?" But we don't always stop to ask ourselves, "How does the customer want to do it?" And we don't always take the essential step of *listening* to customers when they tell us how they want to do something.

Case in point: Virtual (online) complaints that mention your business by name. At one time, these weren't a big deal. If you haven't gotten used to monitoring the Internet for references to your business, you might not realize how important it is to do so now. As it happens, one of the critical best practices advocated by some of the top-performing Ace stores is to monitor the store's social media feedback very closely, and to respond quickly whenever a complaint pops up on one of those interactive channels. You need to pay attention and address whatever issues come up online, because if you don't, that negative feedback may start echoing around cyberspace.

This is an extremely important strategy for thriving and—let's face it— even surviving in the 21st-century marketplace. But Ace stills runs into the occasional owner who asks, "Hey, do I really have to do this?" Guess what the answer is? No. You *don't* have to do it. You don't have to be in business next week, either!

It wasn't all that long ago that Ace faced competitive challenges when competitors like Home Depot, Lowes, and other big-box stores started to invade their communities. If ever there was a time to adapt, this was it. It was no longer "business as usual," as these larger competitors were very aggressive with their prices and advertising. The smart Ace stores adapted to the new competitive landscape by shifting the way they had always done business through changes and tweaks such as extended business hours, being more price competitive, stocking inventory with localized and hard-to-find items, and more.

The moral here, for Ace and for everyone else, is simple: *Adapt or die.* Maybe your daddy didn't have to worry about dealing with the same kind of service, economic, competitive, or communication challenges that you now face. You do! Accept that. Amazement is not an end—not some final answer you come up with once and never revise. It is a process—a journey—that is ongoing, ever-changing, and always being adapted to meet the needs of the current situation.

YOUR AMAZEMENT TOOLBOX

- Times change, and our responsibilities to the customer change too. If we don't adapt, our business may die!

- Amazement is not an end—not some final answer we come up with once and never revise.

- Great customer service is a process that is ongoing, ever-changing. Keep up. You must always adapt.

THE DRILL

- What are the greatest challenges you face in order to stay relevant to your customers?

- How have your customers' expectations and buying habits changed? What have you done to keep up?

6

KNOW THE VALUE OF YOUR CUSTOMERS

Knowing the lifetime value of an average customer can help you make the right customer service decisions.

WHEN EMPLOYEES HAVE CLARITY about the lifetime value of a customer, they can make better decisions during interactions with customers. They are more likely to understand why the service they provide is so important, and they're more likely to be motivated to uphold the shared mission of delivering amazing service.

That mission is not to get rid of the next person in line, not to get to the next break, not to bring the conversation with the customer to its speediest possible conclusion, but to *keep that customer!* When employees, especially those on the front line, have the information they need and are empowered to make appropriate decisions, they're in a much better position to take the steps that help customers decide that they want to come back the next time, every time.

Consider the lifetime value of a customer at a grocery store. Based on several studies, an average customer of a grocery store spends between $80 and $200 each week. To make the math easy, let's say that hypothetically an average family (customer) may visit the store twice a week, spending an average of $50 each time. That's $100 per week for 50 weeks—we'll assume the family takes a two-week vacation. That's about $5,000 each year. Let's say the average family stays in their neighborhood for seven years. That makes the average customer worth about $35,000. That number doesn't factor in any referrals to new families moving into the neighborhood. That means the average customer might be worth multiple times that $35,000. So, if every once in a while a customer complains that a carton of milk was spoiled, do you really want to argue over the price of a carton of milk?

The Five-Dollar Lifeboat strategy from chapter four in part one of this book ties into this. It's such a small amount of money to invest in solving a problem, and it can have such a huge emotional impact on the customer. For most businesses, giving a frontline employee the independent authority to spend five bucks to resolve a problem makes perfect sense. It means giving the employee the authority to hand over another carton of milk in order to resolve a complaint. Why would you want to make the employee leave the customer waiting, even for a moment, while he goes to "check with the manager"? Make it easy for the employee and the customer. Is the customer unhappy? Yes. Would making the customer happy cost less than five bucks? Yes. End of problem. Hand over the carton of milk!

As I point out later in chapter nine (see Tool #40: Satisfaction Is a Rating, Loyalty Is an Emotion), *customer loyalty is all about the next time—every time!* Customers usually have a choice: to do business with us or our competitors. So, what decisions are our employees making *today* that will make our customers decide to do business with us, instead of one of our competitors, the next time they need something we sell? Our employees should be making smart business decisions that allow them to deliver an experience that is so good that, if our customers were to go to a competitor and ask for the same level of service, our competitors would find that customer demanding!

A great example of why you should give your employees all the information they need about lifetime value and margin involves the Ace store in Edgewater, Colorado. This store ran a Labor Day promotion involving a special discount on canning jars, and the offer proved so popular that the store was completely out of stock of the canning jars on the very first day of the promotion. The next day a customer named Tiffany made her way into the store asking for the discounted canning jars. The Ace associate could have just said, "I'm sorry, we ran out of them yesterday." That would have been the easy way out. But she didn't do that. She did a little math. What's the likely lifetime value of the average customer—perhaps this customer? That number was a heck of a lot more than a case of canning jars costs. What's the total cost of securing another box of canning jars for this customer, and discounting them retroactively? A few minutes of my time, plus the discount: less than a few dollars, anyway. Easy call!

At the counter associate's suggestion, the customer got her canning jars, with the full discount, thanks to a special order placed on the spot. They came in after Labor Day, but who cared? "I was taken aback by her going above and beyond," Tiffany recalled later, "and it was much appreciated."

When it comes to creating loyalty, we can't wait until it looks like we are going to lose the loyalty to start trying to keep it. That just doesn't make good business sense! When our people know the numbers, they're more likely to understand *why* loyalty needs to start at the beginning of the process and continue throughout the lifetime of the customer. They're more likely to manage the contact with the customer with that lifetime value in mind every step of the way.

The more we know about the value of a customer, the better the decisions we make about taking care of that customer.

YOUR AMAZEMENT TOOLBOX

- All employees should know the lifetime value of the average customer.

- The more we know about the value of a customer, the better the decisions we make about taking care of that customer.

- Manage the contact with the customer with the lifetime value in mind every step of the way.

THE DRILL

- What do you estimate is the lifetime value of your average customer?

- Think of a time that you solved a problem for a customer that cost a little money in the short term but won the person's loyalty for the long term. Describe what took place.

7

KNOW WHAT DRIVES YOUR SUCCESS

What are the most important factors that drive your business success?

ONE OF THE EXERCISES I do with clients is to ask them to define their most important success drivers. Typically, they will have three to five, maybe six, of these drivers. I then ask them to choose which one driver is the most important. In other words, why would someone do business with them, or choose them over a competitor?

Jay Heubner, Ace's Director of Retail Training, told me that there are five factors that are absolutely critical to an Ace store's success. I didn't have to ask him to come up with them. He already knew them, and one of his goals is to make sure that every single owner, manager, and associate in the Ace family knows exactly what those five keys to success are. The list is Ace's version of a classic marketing concept known as "The Five Ps."

The first P is for PEOPLE. Ace depends on its people to deliver a great experience to customers, and to earn Ace the reputation as the most helpful hardware stores on the planet. They refer to their people as their "weapon in the retail world." Without the right people, trained in the right strategies, supported over time, there's nothing else to talk about.

The second P is for PRODUCT. Ace is recognized as one of the top retailers in the entire industry, so obviously this P is pretty important to them. Each Ace store stocks high-quality products and manages the inventory with the goal of helping the customer get everything he or she needs in a single trip. The retailers localize their inventory with the right local and hard-to-find products to meet the needs of their communities. Simply put, the strategy is to have a relevant, differentiated, and local product mix. And by the way, if the people at your local Ace store don't have the product you need in the store, they will try to get it for you.

The third P is for PRICING. Ace is all about delivering exceptional value for the money paid, and its pricing reflects that. They define value as: competitive price + convenience + quality products + exceptional customer service.

The fourth P is for PLACE. In addition to the convenient neighborhood locations, this factor connects to the physical features of the store itself, and to related aspects of the store experience such as size of the store, parking, fixtures, signage, décor elements, and more. Convenience and the focus on the customer are of the utmost importance.

The fifth and final P is for PROMOTION. This factor has to do with advertising, public relations, special rewards programs for repeat Ace customers, and couponing initiatives. Whether it takes place at the national level or in the local neighborhood, promotion makes a big difference in the marketplace. Ace uses promotion to meet the brand promise of helpful.

Now, if you're an Ace store owner, manager, or associate, you can look at that list and instantly know what the most important areas are for you to focus on if you want your store to survive and thrive.

Your business needs to define what your "Five Ps" are. Of course, they don't have to start with the letter P. They don't all need to start with the same letter. You don't have to have five. It could be just one, or it could be ten. The key is that they are well-thought-out enough to show you where your strengths are. This can't be what you aspire to be. This list has to be about what and who you are.

Notice that Ace's very first P is PEOPLE. People is how Ace delivers on the *helpful* brand promise. No matter how great their product, pricing, place, and promotion are, if the people are there to support these four other Ps and they don't deliver on their brand promise, none of the other Ps matter. Is that one of your strengths? It should be.

Know what you're good at. Be clear about it. And, make sure everyone in your organization, from the most senior executive to the most recent hire, knows and understands your strengths.

YOUR AMAZEMENT TOOLBOX

- Everyone in your organization should know, and be able to discuss, the key factors for success in your marketplace.

- Your list of business success factors should be comprehensive, concise, and easy for people at all levels to understand.

- No matter how good your list of success factors is, if your people don't deliver on your brand promise, none of it matters.

THE DRILL

- What would you say are the five most important reasons a customer would want to do business with you? Which of these factors is *the most* important?

8

YOU CAN'T BE GOOD AT EVERYTHING

Your company can't possibly be excellent at everything it does. And it shouldn't try.

THAT'S THE REFRESHING, realistic message of Dr. Frances Frei, author (with Anne Morriss) of *Uncommon Service: How to Win by Putting Customers at the Core of Your Business* (Harvard Business Review Press, 2012). She argues that to be best in class at something you have to be willing to be worst in class at something else.

This idea is refreshing because, for years, too many of us have gotten caught up in the seductive idea of "achieving excellence" throughout the enterprise, as though excellence were something that we could somehow deliver in every single aspect of our business, for every single customer, internal and external, every single time. Whatever it takes, we tell ourselves, we are committed to achieving excellence in literally everything we do. Is that really the right commitment? Can we really be *best* at everything? Probably not. But we can be the best at what we choose to be known for.

This also means that not all potential customers should be your customers. But the ones that are your customers should be *amazed*, every single time. That is the customer group to focus on. For those customers, we can be best at what they want and expect. But we can't be best at *everything, for everyone, all the time.*

Ace is the perfect example of a company that has put this vitally important strategy into action. There are certain areas where Ace has made the strategic decision to be broadly competitive with its big-box store competitors, but they don't to try to beat them at their own game. For example, Ace recognizes that they can be competitive on things like price and inventory, but downright *excellent* at helpful. What's more, Ace may be recognized as a leader in the general area of "home improvement," but where they really excel is in the areas of maintenance and repair. They *own* that part of the industry. Ace makes the smaller maintenance and repair projects especially easy for you. How do they do that? By focusing like a laser beam on things like convenience, store design, maintaining an inventory of hard-to-find items, and amazing helpful service and expertise.

If you're looking for someone whose expertise will get you across the finish line with your home maintenance or repair project, someone who will help you cross that item off your to-do list, someone who will find a local or hard-to-find item, someone who will give you amazingly helpful service and make you feel absolutely certain that you got more than your money's worth in the process, Ace is the place.

It happened over and over again while I was interviewing Ace people for this book: They told me that the customer who cares about price and nothing else is not at the center of their business plan. That's not their game. While they are competitively or fairly priced, Ace chooses to win on helpful. That's a strategic decision.

So, what are you trying to win on? It's fine to have an aggressive goal, but the reality is that some unrealistic goals that are all about "excellence in everything" can hurt your organization.

As Ace's CEO John Venhuizen told me, "We remind ourselves every day that it is better to differentiate ourselves on something we are already good at—which is *helping* people figure out how best to complete a home improvement or maintenance project—than it is to try to be better at something that the competition is already good at."

YOUR AMAZEMENT TOOLBOX

- Dr. Frances Frei says that to be best in class at one thing, you have to be willing to be worst in class at something else.

- You can't be best at everything. Don't even try. But do be best at something *specific* that your customer wants.

- Identify areas that you *can* excel at and exploit them. Identify areas that you are *not* going to excel at and embrace them.

- Figure out how to be better at something that the competition is not already good at.

THE DRILL

- What does your company do best? What gives—or could give—your company a competitive advantage?

- Is there something your company might not be great at but you make up for with excellence in another area?

9

PLAY TO YOUR STRENGTHS

The best get better by working on their strengths,
not on their weaknesses.

WHILE I WAS TALKING TO DAVID ZIEGLER, the current Chairman of the Board of Ace Hardware and owner of several Ace hardware stores, about what traits made for effective leadership at Ace (and elsewhere), he mentioned the importance of developing a personal growth strategy. Just as a company must focus on its strengths, at the same time choosing what not to focus on, an individual executive needs to decide what he or she will take on as a personal priority and what will be delegated to someone else.

Ace owners have to wear many hats: merchant, accountant, human resource manager, salesperson, etc. The best owners play to their strengths and fill the gaps by hiring people with the right attributes to create a successful business. This ties into the previous tool, You Can't Be Good at Everything. The things you decide to hold on to should relate directly to something that you know you do very well. The things you should, as Mr. Ziegler puts it, "fire yourself from" are those areas in which you are unlikely to develop core strengths.

This is a great reminder that each of us, as an individual, faces an important question. As time passes, are we going to spend more and more of our careers focusing on what we're really good at? Or are we going to spend less time deploying our core strengths, in a misguided attempt to become good at everything? Ace urges its people to choose the first option, and I do too.

If you think that this approach applies only to members of the executive team, you'd be wrong. It shows up throughout the organization. It's true that when you start in at the entry level with Ace (or any other employer, for that matter), you have to be ready to do whatever you're asked to do. But after just a little time on the job, what you're going to find is that you have a strong aptitude and interest for certain parts of the business, and less aptitude and interest in other parts.

Like a lot of customer- and employee-centric companies, Ace believes that an associate has the responsibility to share with his or her manager where the passion is, where the energy is, and where the motivation is. It's nice if the manager is able to figure this out independently, but it's even better if the associate makes a point of sitting down at some point with his or her manager and saying something like this: "Hey, I have an associate degree in horticulture, and I love landscaping. I've been thinking that it might make more sense for me to spend some time over in the Lawn and Garden department, where I can really help out, rather than to stay where I am in Hardware. What do you think?"

Marcus Buckingham makes a very strong case for playing to your strengths in his mega-bestselling book *Go Put Your Strengths to Work* (Free Press, 2007). Conventional wisdom says to work hard and train to overcome your personal weaknesses. However, a study of 80,000 managers in more than 400 companies found that the best managers believe that the opposite is true. You might be able to help a person get better in a deficient area, but if you try to help them get better at what they are already good at, you move them from being good toward being *really* good—and maybe even toward greatness.

The bottom line: Get better at what you already do well. Know and play to your strengths!

YOUR AMAZEMENT TOOLBOX

- Develop a personal growth strategy that plays to your strengths.

- If you are a manager, decide what items on your to-do list do not play to your strengths and can be delegated to others.

- Conventional wisdom says to work on your weaknesses. The best people know it's better to work on improving your strengths.

- If you're a frontline employee, talk to your manager about supporting your company in ways that connect to your strengths.

THE DRILL

- What is your greatest personal and professional strength?

- What are you doing now (or plan to do) to develop that strength even more?

CHAPTER SEVEN

CULTURE

"The culture is made—or destroyed—by its articulate voices."

—AYN RAND

THE CULTURE DEFINES THE BUSINESS. And culture starts with you. Your job is to be an articulate voice.

Why focus time and attention on your company's culture? Because most, if not all, companies that fail to amaze the customer have failed to amaze the employee. The two challenges are always linked together. In this chapter, you learn how to address that challenge, and why it is everyone's job to do so.

The next thirteen Amazement Tools (#s 10–22) will help you create and sustain a culture that is customer- and employee-focused. It is up to you to do your part in setting the example and maintaining that culture. You have the power to create it and sustain that positive culture—or, if you choose not to manage it well, to erode it. Culture always starts on the inside, with you. And whatever the culture is on the inside of your organization, it is going to be felt on the outside by the customer.

Culture Tools

10. To Be the Best Place to Buy, Be the Best Place to Work

11. Don't Take the Easy Way Out

12. The Awesome Responsibility

13. Defend the Culture

14. Shift Your Vocabulary

15. Adopt a Customer-First Mindset

16. Celebrate Uniqueness

17. Great Ideas Come from Everyone

18. Consistency

19. Tell the Story

20. Be a Committed Learner

21. Mentoring

22. Starting Over

10

TO BE THE BEST PLACE TO BUY, BE THE BEST PLACE TO WORK

Treat your employees the way you want your customers to be treated—maybe even better!

I'VE BEEN SHARING THE SENTENCE you just read with audiences since at least the mid-1980s, and every time I say those words out loud, I always see lots of people in the audience nodding their heads in agreement. In fact, audience members often tell me that this one sentence is one of the most memorable and important parts of my program. It's my customer service slant to the familiar Golden Rule: "Do unto others as you would have them do unto you." I call it the Employee Golden Rule. I have yet to meet a business leader who disagrees with this concept.

Yet the reality is that many companies whose leaders *tell* me that they agree wholeheartedly with what you just read *do not* treat their employees the way they want the customers treated. The end result is that their customers are potentially not treated as well as they could be.

So, why don't they follow through on the Employee Golden Rule? The answer starts with the company's culture.

First and foremost, the company must get into *alignment* (which I discussed in chapter four, "Operationalizing Helpful"). Leadership must determine the direction in which they want to lead the culture. If the goal is a truly customer-focused culture, then it must start at the top, with a mission and vision that are not only created but also implemented throughout the entire company. And, the vision and the mission must be crystal clear. They are what I referred to earlier in this book as the mantra, a simplistic one-sentence—or shorter—version of the mission and vision of the company. By now you know Ace's mantra is one word: Helpful.

Until the company and every employee has a mantra to live by, and leadership sets the example of how to live and defend that mantra, the internal culture may be out of alignment.

Without a mantra, without a cultural touch point, without a point on the compass that everyone can use as a guide, without at least one role model who walks the walk for the rest of the enterprise, there can be no customer-first culture. If there is no shared, perpetually reinforced understanding of "how we do things here," no real-world standard that *actually rewards* treating both internal and external customers well, it's all just talk.

In fact, just talking about it in this culture hurts your organization. You have to connect the words to the actions. Once you have a mantra—such as "helpful"—someone must model it until it becomes part of the company's DNA, *as experienced by the employees.*

That's the only way you can possibly amaze your customers every time—by amazing your employees first, so that they treat each other the way they want the customer treated. When it comes to amazing customer service, it starts on the inside and works its way out, and everyone in the company has to step up and become a leader in that effort.

Amazing from the inside out means not saying one thing and doing something else. It means being genuine, and making sure that what people see and hear from you is what they actually get from you. So at Ace, associates *experience helpful* before they are expected to *generate helpful.*

What does that mean in practice? It means you build your community from the inside out, which means you start with the employees.

Matt Dowdell, an Ace owner from Montana, told me that his personal mission is to be the best employer within a 10-mile radius of his store. He wants people to line up to not just work in his store, but to have a career in his store. That mission affects his hiring judgments, his compensation plan, his training routine, and of course, his interactions with his associates on a day-to-day basis. (By the way, he also wanted to be the best charitable contributor to the community within a 10-mile radius, and of course, the most recommended hardware store within a 10-mile radius.) That's building *helpful* from the inside out!

This approach is what I have referred to as *employee centricity*. If the concept of customer centricity is a focus of all activities supporting and benefiting the customer, then employee centricity is where it starts.

Until we have a mantra that everyone agrees on internally, we don't really have an employee-centric enterprise. And until we achieve that, we really can't have a customer-centric enterprise. That's because the internal customer experience determines the external customer experience. Telling people how to treat customers is one thing. *Showing* how you want them treated, by modeling the behavior with them that you want employees to display toward the customer, is completely different.

As Mark Schulein, one of the Ace retailers told me, "We focus on engaging with our own people first, knowing what they're going through at home, finding out what's going on in their lives, learning what we can do to support them, because that's exactly what we want them to do for the customer once the customer walks through the door. We believe that in order to be the best place to shop you have to be the best place to work first."

Remember: Whatever gets rewarded and reinforced becomes part of the company's culture—and whatever *doesn't* get rewarded and reinforced affects the culture too.

YOUR AMAZEMENT TOOLBOX

- Treat employees the way you want the customer treated, maybe even better.

- The only way you can possibly amaze your customers every time is by amazing your employees first.

- Talking about the Employee Golden Rule is not enough. You, as a leader, must model it daily.

- A mantra is a simplistic one-sentence, or shorter, version of the mission and vision of the company.

- Every employee must buy into and live by the mantra, and it starts with leadership setting the example of how to do so.

- The internal customer experience determines the external customer experience.

- Everyone can be a leader when it comes to customer service.

THE DRILL

- What does it mean to "Treat employees the way you want your customers to be treated—maybe even better"? Share an example.

11

DON'T TAKE THE EASY WAY OUT

"There's no traffic jam on the extra mile."

LOTS OF PEOPLE CLAIM to have been the first to say the quote that appears above—I like to attribute it to the late Zig Ziglar—but regardless of whoever said it first, it means the same thing: *Don't take the easy way out.*

This principle could correspond to a number of important relationship goals with the customer. For instance, being helpful, learning to say "Yes" instead of "No," creating customer evangelists, building and sustaining long-term loyalty, and so on. Those are all outcomes. Ultimately, I think the most important reason to instill this principle is that it reminds your organization how important it is to *capitalize on the precious opportunity to create a Moment of Magic with each specific customer request.*

Many of your competitors won't do that. They'll miss that precious opportunity, and probably not even recognize it in the first place. That's human nature. They may even see a customer's special request as a nuisance. Most of the time, they'll take the easy way out and find some way to get out of having to deal with that request.

If you do business the way Ace does, though, you'll build a culture that *never* takes the easy way out, whether internally or externally.

This may all sound a little abstract, so let me show you exactly what that kind of culture looks like in action. What you're about to read is a verbatim email from a happy Ace customer. Notice that the email is extremely long and detailed, and that the customer who took the time to write it is now an evangelist for Ace!

SUBJECT: Outstanding Customer Service

It seems that too often nowadays, the only time a business hears from a customer is when there is a complaint. But that's not why I'm sending you this message. Instead, I'd like to let you know how pleased I am with service that I recently received from your employee, Josh.

A couple of weeks ago, I decided that my 9-year-old lawnmower had seen its better days. My daughter and also my brother-in-law had both recently purchased Toro personal pace lawnmowers. One was from Ace Hardware in Apple Valley; the other from a Minneapolis Ace Hardware. They seemed pleased with the mower so I thought it would be a good model for me as well.

I called Pellicci Ace Hardware and talked with Josh. He was very informative, and even though there were no Toro personal pace mowers in the store, he quickly made a call to the local Toro representative. And if I recall correctly, I had a new mower within one day.

Now, I have a small car, so there's no way I could have transported the mower. But Josh delivered it—no charge. Talk about fast, excellent service!

However, we soon discovered that the mower that had been delivered wasn't a good fit for me. I am 4 feet 11 inches tall, and the handlebars were just way too high, and on that particular model, the handlebars cannot be adjusted. I mentioned this in the call I made to the Ace store. Josh came by and picked up the mower. Again, at no charge.

Back to the drawing board we went. He called me within a short time and informed me of another Toro model personal pace that had three adjustable heights for the handlebar. And the next day, Josh called to say that he had received the mower in the store and would deliver it that afternoon and again, no delivery charge.

Josh was ever so patient with me throughout the entire transaction, and he politely answered all of the questions I had. And if he didn't have an answer, he offered to find out and get back to me—which he always did in a timely fashion. It's been a long time since I've received such superb customer service. Not only did Josh respond quickly, but he followed up after I had used the mower to ensure everything was all right.

So because of my recent experience with Josh's service, let's just say I'm convinced: Pellicci Ace Hardware is the place! Thank you to Josh for his outstanding customer service attitude!

Sincerely,
Judy

Of course, there were multiple opportunities for Moments of Magic within this remarkable story, and it's easy to get excited about how well Josh capitalized on them all. The willingness to deliver the lawnmower, not once, but twice. The no-hassle exchange. The follow-up to make sure everything was all right. Yet, what I want you to notice is that it all began with *one* fateful moment: The moment when the customer called and asked whether or not the store had a Toro Personal Pace lawnmower.

Think about it. Nine times out of ten, if you called a store and asked them for an item they didn't sell, you would probably hear something like, "I'm sorry, we don't stock that item. You might try a different store."

It's easy to say "No" to a special request. It's more convenient to *not* take extra time and effort to take care of a customer. It's easy to be like most everyone else, nothing special. It's easy to create average Moments of Truth—also known as Moments of Mediocrity. In other words, it's easy to take the easy way out.

The best and the brightest, like Josh in the example above, are different. They *don't* take the easy way out.

YOUR AMAZEMENT TOOLBOX

- Capitalize on the precious opportunity to create a Moment of Magic with each customer request.

- A customer's special request is not a nuisance; it is an opportunity to show how good you are.

- The best and the brightest don't take the easy way out when a customer asks for help!

THE DRILL

- Think of a time when you *could* have told a customer that you couldn't help, but you chose to make the effort—even though it might have been a little inconvenient—to take care of the customer. What did you do, and what happened as a result?

12

THE AWESOME RESPONSIBILITY

To the customer, you are the company!

CUSTOMERS DON'T DO BUSINESS with a company. They do business with the people who work for the company. Perhaps a better way to say this would be that customers *interact* with the people who work for a company.

One day I took my kids to breakfast at a fast-food restaurant. The moment we walked in we were greeted by a wonderful woman who welcomed us and took our order. As she completed the transaction, she talked to my kids and asked them about school. She came back with our food, thanked us, and told us to have a great day. On the way out of the restaurant, my daughter said, "The people at this restaurant are so nice."

What did she mean when she said *the people*? We only interacted with one person! However, that person, at least to my daughter, represented the entire restaurant—all of the employees and the brand.

Think about it. People will sometimes say, "I love doing business with them . . ." In reality, they may be talking about a he or a she—just one person. And, here is the point. At any given time one person represents everything about your organization. It's an *awesome responsibility*!

Every employee in your company carries an awesome responsibility: being your company. To the customer, that employee doesn't just "represent" your company. He or she *is* the entire company, every working moment. Any interaction that affects a customer, consciously or not, forms an impression. That's the Moment of Truth we covered in chapter five. Hopefully that interaction isn't a Moment of Misery or a Moment of Mediocrity. You want it to always be a Moment of Magic, better than average.

An Ace owner, Mark Schulein from Southern California, told me that his store was only as strong as the "weakest link" employee in the building. Why? Because the interaction that any given customer has with that weakest link employee *forms the customer's impression of the entire store.* So if the weakest link is in a bad mood when the customer happens to ask a question, and the customer picks up on that, the whole store was rude to that customer. In that scenario, it doesn't matter how good everyone else is when it comes to interacting with customers. The weakest link undermines everyone else's work. That's why Mark's ongoing training goal was to make sure that the weakest link point of contact in the store still delivered an amazing experience, every time.

YOUR AMAZEMENT TOOLBOX

- At any given time, one person represents everything about your organization. It's an awesome responsibility!

- To the customer, an employee doesn't just "represent" your company. He or she is your company.

- In amazing organizations, even the employee who is the "weakest link" should still deliver amazing service.

THE DRILL

- Think of a time when you interacted with a customer in such a way that the customer developed a positive impression about not just you but the entire company. What did you do to make that customer "love" you and the company?

13

DEFEND THE CULTURE

You are part of a team that delivers amazement. Intervene tactfully with colleagues who inadvertently take down that culture!

A WHILE BACK, I was speaking at a conference in Texas. Although I had already checked out of my hotel room, I wanted to take the hotel's shuttle to the airport, which was less expensive than taking a cab. The trouble was, the recently hired front-desk clerk was hung up on the "operations" part of her job. According to the employee manual she'd been given, the shuttle was only for guests of the hotel. Apparently, they'd had a problem with people who weren't guests of the hotel taking advantage of the service. The hotel's solution was to make sure the person on the shuttle was also a registered guest, and the best way to do that was to charge the fee to the guest's room. Unfortunately, I had already checked out of my room, and therefore I no longer had a room to charge to. Technically, that meant I was no longer a guest at the hotel.

I tried my level best to explain to the clerk that I really *was* a guest—I just happened to be one who had checked out of the hotel, apparently a little too early for my own good! She could only repeat what the manual told her: If there was no room account open to charge to, she couldn't let me on the van. There was nothing in the manual about letting me pay cash for the ride, so in her mind, she couldn't do that.

Clearly, this was a Moment of Misery in the making. Fortunately, there was another hotel employee observing this interaction. He tactfully helped his newly hired coworker by telling her that it was okay to accept cash. In the process, he taught her to change her "operations" outlook to a "customer" outlook. A customer-centric culture rewards using your own best judgment in delivering a Moment of Magic, every time!

I got my ride to the airport!

There are a number of amazement lessons that could come out of this story. It could be about common sense, about using your best judgment, about how policies should be considered guidelines and not rules, or any number of other critical principles. What's more, she obviously had not been exposed to Tool #29: One to Say Yes, Two to Say No.

Here's the main thing I want you to notice about the story. When the new front-desk clerk's veteran colleague stepped in, he was doing more than just teaching his colleague that it was okay to accept cash. He was also teaching her to get out of a by-the-book "operations-centric" mindset. He was *defending a customer-centric culture.*

This story shows how one employee intervened to help another employee, and in the process, helped protect the hotel's customer-focused culture. Sometimes it's not easy. Sometimes it's more than just teaching or mentoring. Sometimes you have to "tactfully intervene" when there is a need to defend the culture.

Art Freedman is an Ace store owner in California. In addition to his day-to-day responsibilities, he is also one of Ace Hardware's go-to guys for training and consulting. Art travels all over the world helping other Ace retailers, and he shared a great example of how he once had to defend the Ace culture.

Art noticed a customer who had walked into an Ace store and tried and failed to catch the attention of one of the associates. The customer gave up and headed down the aisle to try to find whatever he was looking for—all because that associate had been busy socializing with another employee.

Art saw it all, and he knew that the associate had failed at a lot more than making eye contact. He had failed to greet the customer, and worse yet, had failed to ask how he could help the customer. He was taking down Ace's culture!

Art quickly intervened. He took that associate aside and tactfully talked to him about what had just happened. He let him know in no uncertain terms that the store, his job, and all of his fellow associates' jobs depended on him executing his responsibility, which was to greet customers when they come in the store, interact with them, notice when they needed help, and deliver on the helpful promise.

Art's a great coach, and when he was finished with his lesson, not only did the employee not repeat his mistake, he also became a defender of Ace's customer-centric culture!

The culture your organization lives by depends on the willingness of you and every one of your employees to live it and defend it.

YOUR AMAZEMENT TOOLBOX

- An *operations-centric culture* is all about following instructions to the letter, even when that means delivering a Moment of Misery.

- A *customer-centric culture* rewards using your own best judgment in delivering a Moment of Magic, every time!

- Coaching and mentoring are great ways of tactfully intervening to "defend" the company's culture.

- Praise and reward the people in your company who defend your customer-centric culture.

- Give people permission to intervene when they notice a colleague inadvertently taking down your customer-centric culture.

- The culture of your organization depends on the willingness of every employee to not just live the culture but also to defend it.

THE DRILL

- Was there ever a time when you witnessed a colleague doing something that seemed to you to undermine your company's positive culture? What did you do? Or, looking back, what do you *wish* you had done?

14

SHIFT YOUR VOCABULARY

Sometimes changing the words you use can change your attitude—and your company's culture.

WORDS HAVE TREMENDOUS POWER. Whenever we choose to change the words we use, we can also change the service culture of the entire organization. We can change the reason we show up for work in the morning. We can change the way we look at our relationships with customers. We can change our business outcomes. We can change everything!

My business coach, Dan Sullivan, doesn't have "clients." Instead, he refers to me—and everyone else who pays to work with him—as a "Multiplier!" This is a conscious choice of Dan's. He calls us "Multipliers" because he has a "Multiplier Mindset" when it comes to me and everyone else he coaches. He tries to multiply our free time, our business results, and lots of other things that he knows we want to have abundantly in our lives. Dan's pretty good at multiplying!

By the way, he also views us as Multiplier on his behalf—advocates who can evangelize for his services and bring him in more business. And you know what? He's absolutely right about that. We get great results from our relationship with Dan, and we really are more than happy to serve as his Multipliers!

How can you change your vocabulary? You might start by looking closely at the way you refer to customers. There are plenty of companies out there whose employees make a habit of referring to the customer as "Boss." I love that! What a great way to remind yourself, and everyone in your company, about who's really paying your salary, paying your insurance, and keeping the company running. And did you notice that, when you go to one of the Disney theme parks you're never referred to as a "customer"— you're a "Guest," with a capital G? The people who take care of you aren't "employees," either—they're "cast members"! These word choices are not accidents. They are conscious choices that affect the customer relationship and the customer experience in a positive way. In the same way, referring to Ace employees as "associates" changes the dynamic in a positive way.

It doesn't stop there. Like a lot of Ace retailers, Smith's Ace Hardware in Princeton, New Jersey, makes a habit of calling the people they serve "our neighbors." What a game-changer! This one simple vocabulary change totally transforms the relationship. What's the difference between a neighbor and a customer? Well, neighbors look out for each other. Neighbors keep an eye out for each other's best interests. Neighbors care about each other beyond a one-time transaction. Remember the old advice to "love thy neighbor"?

I've had people tell me that this kind of vocabulary change doesn't make a difference. That's true if the terminology change is just the "theme of the week" and doesn't stick. But, if it represents a long-term commitment that helps to define the culture, it works. If you think calling someone a "neighbor" rather than a "customer" during team meetings, strategy sessions, and store encounters is a superficial change, a piece of "happy talk" that can't possibly be expected to affect the bottom line, please permit me to disagree. Once you make a habit of it, this one simple change possibly can transform your business and your career.

Language changes behavior! What we say affects what we think, and what we think affects the way we treat each other. When we call someone across the counter a "neighbor" rather than a "customer," we're sharing something special. Is it crazy to call that special something "love"? Not if your customers return the love! The ones out in Princeton, New Jersey, do. One of them wrote this online about Smith's Ace Hardware: "BEST hardware store EVER. ABSOLUTE BEST SERVICE. If it's possible to LOVE a hardware store, I LOVE this store!"

That's not a customer talking. That's a *neighbor.*

YOUR AMAZEMENT TOOLBOX

- When we choose to change the words we use, we can change the service culture of the entire organization.

- What we say affects what we think, and what we think affects the way we treat each other. Language changes behavior!

- Is there another word you can use to describe your customer, such as Guest or Neighbor? How about a word to describe your employees?

- Calling someone across the counter a "neighbor" rather than a "customer" can make them feel special.

THE DRILL

- How do you refer to your customers? Do you call them customers, or members, or guests, or *neighbors*? Is there another positive word that you could use to refer to your customers? If so, what would it be?

15

ADOPT A CUSTOMER-FIRST MINDSET

Everyone—and I do mean everyone—in your organization affects the customer experience.

IN TODAY'S WORLD, you are courting disaster if you think that the customer service department is the only area involved in customer service. Each and every individual in your organization is, in reality, his or her own customer service department! The trouble is, not everyone in the enterprise always realizes this.

Whether you are a clerk in the accounting department or you are a sales rep on the floor or you are making a contribution anywhere else in the organization, you have customers, and you are involved in customer service. Something you do affects a customer—whether that customer is internal or external. Jan Carlzon of Scandinavian Airlines said, "If you're not directly servicing the customer, you are supporting someone who is." So if you take your eye off the ball and ignore your service responsibility for too long, some external customer is eventually going to defect to the competition!

And now you also run the risk that the disappointed customer will head to Facebook, Twitter, Google Plus, or whatever new channel has just opened up, and use that platform to tell everyone on earth exactly why he or she defected!

Can you see now why everyone in your organization has to adopt a "customer first" mindset?

Years ago I attended some courses offered by Disney. They teach that every employee (Disney calls them "cast members") at a Disney theme park has three jobs:

1. To do the job they were hired to do.

2. To take care of the Guest. (This is the one that makes every job a customer service job, regardless of someone's responsibility.)

3. To keep the park clean.

This can apply to every company. Maybe you don't have to worry about No. 3, keeping the park clean—the word "park" being a metaphor for whatever your business is. But, the other two strategies are rock solid. Everybody has at least two jobs: Do the job they are hired to do and to take care of the customer.

The people at Ace, like the other great service organizations out there, are masters at this concept. They know that *everyone, regardless of job title,* ultimately affects the external customer experience. That means *everyone* has to deliver on *helpful,* every time, in every interaction, with everyone else. No excuses. No kidding. That's just how they do business!

My favorite expression of this value comes from Ace owner Matt Dowdell in Montana, who tells everyone on his staff, "We've got a lot of fancy machinery in the front of the store, and we've got a lot of fancy machinery in the back of the store . . . but if any one of us ever forgets that the point of all that machinery is to help Joe take care of his Honey-Do list, and to make Joe's day a little easier, none of it matters." No matter what machinery you're using, or where you're using it, you'd better be using it to make life easier for Joe! That value drives everything Ace does. And, it is everyone's job, regardless of their job description, to *always* keep the customer in mind. That's a customer-first mindset.

YOUR AMAZEMENT TOOLBOX

- No matter what you do in the company, you affect the customer experience.

- You actually have two jobs: the one you were hired to do, and to take care of the customer.

- If you're not dealing with the customer, you are supporting someone who is.

THE DRILL

- How do your job and responsibilities directly and indirectly impact the customer experience?

- Are you supporting someone else who deals directly with the customer? If so, who? And how do you support that person?

16

CELEBRATE UNIQUENESS

Respect the different personalities of the people and teams who fulfill your brand promise.

IN SOME OF THE TRAINING PROGRAMS we create for our clients, we do a team-building exercise we call *The Great Alphabet Game*. We have a room full of a company's employees sitting at round tables. The rules are that each group has to come up with 26 different items, each item beginning with a different letter of the alphabet. They can use whatever is in their pockets, purses, briefcases, etc. The first team that gets an item for each of the 26 letters wins.

It's interesting how quickly a team wins, and how close most of the other teams were to getting all 26 objects. What's even more interesting is that the different teams use all kinds of different strategies and still come close to winning. Some will start by throwing a bunch of "stuff" into the middle of the table. Others take a more orderly approach by taking out a sheet of paper and writing all 26 letters in a neat column before they begin to search for their items. What's also astonishing is the sheer variety of the objects that people carry around with them. Talk about diversity!

The lessons from this exercise are important. First, there are lots of different ways to accomplish the same goal. The activity also proves that diversity and uniqueness in a team is a big advantage. There is no way that any of these teams could have won if it was just one or two people playing against a table of eight. The greater the number of different, unique approaches you incorporate, the better off you are.

There are certain key concepts you will find emphasized at Ace Hardware stores. For instance: Helpful. Trusted. Consistent. Those are core attributes of the Ace experience. They're part of the brand. If you don't try to deliver on those promises, both internally and externally, then you haven't yet figured out what Ace is all about. Every single store buys into helpful, trusted, and consistent and accepts the responsibility of reinforcing those values with both management and associates. And, while every store celebrates their values, they also celebrate each *person's* uniqueness.

As Kane Calamari, Ace Hardware's Corporate Vice President of Retail Operations and New Business, put it, "If I had to pick one thing that other businesses could learn from Ace, it would be the celebration of uniqueness. While we love consistency and we love our brand, an important part of our business model is our respect for each store's unique personality and unique approach. That's what allows us to localize and imbed in the community: a willingness to let each store fulfill the brand promise in its own way. It's the same at the individual level. You have lots of different people, lots of different skill sets, lots of different personalities, all committed to the same brand promise."

Each Ace store is deeply individualized, and each Ace associate brings a different set of personal skills and experiences to the table. An Ace store in northern Maine may take a totally different approach to promotion, inventory selection, and a dozen other areas than a store in Southern California does. It has to! It serves, and is part of, a very different community! I doubt you'll find any snow blowers in San Diego. Ace respects that, because it has built diversity into its business plan in a powerful way.

Celebrate your organization's diversity and uniqueness, both at the organizational and the personal level.

YOUR AMAZEMENT TOOLBOX

- Agree on the core elements of the brand promise, then let people and teams fulfill it using their own unique personalities.

- Build diversity into your business plan. Different people and different ideas can be a tremendous advantage.

- Celebrate your enterprise's diversity and uniqueness, both at the organizational and the personal level.

THE DRILL

- What makes your company unique?

- What have you done to make your company unique?

- Describe a time when a colleague successfully solved a customer problem by taking a very different approach than you would have taken.

17

GREAT IDEAS
COME FROM EVERYONE

Share the breakthroughs that make amazing service possible. Don't keep them to yourself.

EMPLOYEES FROM ALL AREAS of a business, and especially the ones on the front line, are involved in solving problems and being helpful. The corporate culture should encourage employees to come up with new and cool ideas, either on their own or as a result of their interactions with customers. The question is, do you have a culture that fosters those creative ideas, and when there are good ideas, what becomes of them?

It's much more common than company leaders realize that employees come up with potentially awesome ideas but never tell anyone about them. In fact, if I had to bet, I'd bet that the majority of employees who have customer-facing responsibilities fall into this category. They don't tell anybody about the idea, they just came up with. They don't tell anyone about the great idea that a customer just shared with them. Why? Well, there are a whole lot of possible reasons for this reluctance—ranging from a simple lack of encouragement on the part of management to a well-placed fear that other people will think an unorthodox idea is dumb. But there are no *good* reasons not to share ideas, especially ideas that arise from your interactions with customers!

The simplest way around this problem is to make a conscious effort to elicit suggestions from the front lines, and to acknowledge and reward those ideas that do become best practices for your organization. The rewards can involve anything that is meaningful to employees, ranging from appropriate recognition to time off to financial rewards for the very best ideas. Usually, though, the positive regard of peers is a strong enough incentive to get the process started.

Managers can do their part to support an innovative, idea-friendly working culture by (a) never, ever criticizing an idea in a public setting, and (b) creating easy-to-access tools for capturing ideas from both employees and customers. Just remember: The number of great ideas your organization gets from its employees depends on the way management responds to mediocre ideas! If an employee is humiliated for sharing what others consider a "dumb" idea, what's his or her incentive to come up with a better one?

Employees can contribute to an innovative culture by praising and properly crediting the good ideas of their peers. Never take credit for someone else's breakthrough! This stifles innovation and causes other cultural problems too.

Some companies have a brief weekly, and in some cases daily, ritual for sharing recent challenges and "brainstorming" possible solutions to them. These weekly or daily "huddles" are a fertile source of (among other things) good ideas that can improve any organization.

Brian Ziegler, president of a number of Ace Hardware stores in the Chicago, Illinois, area, has a brilliant way to garner new and innovative ideas. Brian has a "Lunch with the President" program in which there is a designated day of the month that all employees who have a birthday that month are invited to lunch at a local restaurant. Each employee is required to share an idea that will improve the organization. These lunches are an excellent communication tool for upper management to use to listen to all staff members. Each month the ideas are summarized and management reports back to each employee as to what happened with his or her idea.

This kind of program can be adapted to any type of business, large or small. For larger companies it may be the vice president or a manager of a department who meets with the employees for lunch. The key is to create a culture that encourages and embraces the ideas and opinions of employees.

YOUR AMAZEMENT TOOLBOX

- Many employees come up with potentially awesome ideas, but they never tell anyone about them.

- Make a conscious effort to elicit suggestions; acknowledge and reward ideas that become best practices.

- Properly credit the good ideas of your peers.

- Consider a weekly or daily "huddle" ritual for sharing recent challenges and brainstorming possible solutions.

- A "Lunch with the Boss" program is an excellent way to connect with employees and get great ideas to improve the company.

THE DRILL

- Have you ever come up with a new or different way to do your job? What was it? Did you share the idea with others?

- Does your company have a process to elicit suggestions from employees and customers?

- What is the best such idea you have ever heard?

18

CONSISTENCY

What does it take to build intense customer loyalty? One of the key strategies is basic, but powerful: PREDICTABLE CONSISTENCY!

BRAND LOYALTY DEPENDS ON three interrelated quality service experiences. They are as follows:

Brand loyalty prerequisite No. 1: First and foremost, the product or service has to work. That's really no surprise. If the quality isn't there, you're in trouble.

Brand loyalty prerequisite No. 2: This is about how well you deliver the product or service that you sell. The customer service level needs to be above average. Notice that the service level doesn't have to be a wow experience every time in order to deliver loyalty to your brand. It just needs to be above average.

Brand loyalty prerequisite No. 3: There has to be confidence in the consumer's mind that No. 1 and No. 2 above will happen predictably into the future. In other words, there has to be consistency. Confidence comes from the customer knowing what to expect—and getting it. The experience becomes predictable.

As mentioned, all three of these prerequisites are interrelated. It's like a three-legged stool. Take away one of the legs, and the stool tips over. No matter how nice you are (customer service), if the product doesn't consistently do what it is supposed to do, you will probably lose the customer. No matter how well the product or service works (quality), if the service experience you deliver isn't consistently above average, you are vulnerable to a competitor who does deliver that kind of experience.

Inconsistency can be a "loyalty killer." (For more about this subject, see Tool #37: Avoid Loyalty Killers.) Customers like consistency. They like what they are used to. That means you have to create confidence, and confidence comes from a predictable experience. You want customers to *own* their experience with you, which means that they have to know what to expect—all of the time!

I work with a lot of business leaders, and it always surprises me how totally focused some of them can be on loyalty prerequisites 1 and 2, but not always at the same time. That's where No. 3 comes in. They are committed to product quality. They understand the importance of above-average service. But sometimes they don't connect the dots, so the customer doesn't always have a consistent experience. By the way, it's usually No. 2, the customer service, where the inconsistency shows up.

One of the things Ace does really well is connect the dots. It works very hard to stock a good product and create a service experience that is beyond compare. That doesn't mean customers never experience service problems. Like any business with a pulse, it occasionally delivers Moments of Misery. But when those Moments of Misery do happen, customers tend to give Ace the benefit of the doubt. They have had enough above-average experiences in the past that they now have confidence that whatever problem they've just run into will be resolved to their satisfaction . . . *because that's what usually happens*! That's a very important point to remember. Consistency doesn't mean you never have a problem. It means that if there ever is a problem, your customers have confidence in you to deliver a positive outcome.

As Doug, an Ace customer in Washington, D.C., put it, "I want to know how these guys hire their staff. I've been going there for three years, and every single time I've been in—about three dozen times—I've received absolutely excellent service."

YOUR AMAZEMENT TOOLBOX

- No matter how nice you are, if the product doesn't *consistently* do what it is supposed to, you'll probably lose the customer.

- No matter how good your product/service is, if your service isn't *consistently* above average, you'll probably lose the customer.

- Inconsistency is a Loyalty Killer.

- You have to create confidence, and confidence comes from a predictable positive experience.

- You want customers to own their experience with you. They have to know what to expect, all of the time!

- Consistency doesn't mean you never have a problem. It means your customers can count on you if ever there is a problem.

THE DRILL

- Customers love consistency. What can your customers count on receiving from you the first time—and every time—without exception?

- How would your customers finish this sentence: "I can always count on them to . . ."?

19

TELL THE STORY

The stories that are created between a business and its customers can drive the culture.

PERHAPS YOU'VE HEARD THE FAMOUS STORY of the Nordstrom's employee who gave a customer a refund on a set of tires. Nordstrom's return policy is very liberal, but it has never sold tires! Even so, the employee still refunded the customer's money. Or maybe you've heard the story of how the call service representative at Zappos.com helped a customer order a pizza. Zappos.com doesn't sell pizza . . . but that didn't stop the call center rep from finding a restaurant in the customer's city that would deliver a pizza.

The story behind the Nordstrom's story is that the gentleman returning the tires insisted that he'd bought them from that store. Actually, he had—before it became a Nordstrom's. Right location, wrong store! You can agree or disagree, but this was enough of a reason for the employee to give him a refund on the tires. So a customer service legend was born.

There's a story behind the Zappos.com pizza story too. It was a test. Zappos.com sells shoes and fashion accessories from a website, and is famous for its customer service. CEO Tony Hsieh wanted to see just how customer friendly his call center reps were. So he had someone call and ask the rep to help find him a place to get a late-night pizza. The Zappos.com employee passed with flying colors, giving the "customer" three different restaurant options.

These stories—and companies—are now classics in the customer service world. Admittedly, these stories have been overused, but there is a reason for that. They make their point. They are extreme examples of core values of a company that have turned into legends and help to drive the culture of these companies.

You don't have to have publicly recognized stories or legends to put this tool to use. However, using true above-and-beyond stories that you get from a customer's letter or an online review can help create an internal legend that gives employees something to aspire to and emulate, while helping to shape your company's culture.

That's exactly what Ace Hardware has done. Once you spend some quality time behind the scenes, you realize that *the whole enterprise is driven by stories*. Specifically, it's driven by true stories of helpful encounters with customers.

I've already shared many of the awesome "tribal narratives" from Ace, but I saved a special one for this chapter, a true story that perfectly illustrates what Ace is all about and what helpful is all about. Here it is.

Joe Rutter, an Ace manager from Knoxville, Tennessee, tells of a visit from a favorite loyal customer whom I'll call Mrs. Wilson. Now, Mrs. Wilson was in her mid-80s at the time she made this visit to the local Ace store. She made that visit during an intense heat wave, when the heat index had climbed above 110 degrees. Even though the media posted warnings about the dangers of going outside, Mrs. Wilson still ventured out to the store.

She took a taxi. When she walked in the door, Joe noticed right away that Mrs. Wilson didn't look at all well. She seemed flushed, she was sweating, and she was disoriented. She didn't seem to know what she was doing. She couldn't seem to remember why she had taken the cab to get to Joe's store.

Joe and a couple of associates sat her down on a nearby bench just to let her collect herself, and sat with her, hoping to help her reorient herself. After just a few minutes, though, it became obvious that she was still confused. What to do?

Mrs. Wilson had no ride home, and no family in the area that anyone could call to have her picked up. Joe's best guess was that the heat had gotten to her, and that she just needed to go home and rest. As it happened, he knew where she lived, because he'd made several deliveries to her house.

Joe offered to drive Mrs. Wilson home, and she accepted the offer. Whatever it was that she had meant to buy at Ace could wait until next time.

Joe drove Mrs. Wilson back home—but he had to make a detour. As they were approaching her neighborhood in his nice, cool car, she regained some of that composure she had lost in the heat—and remembered that she needed a loaf of bread. Would Joe mind stopping by the store so she could pick that up?

Joe didn't mind at all.

Now, you could put up all kinds of posters about helpful, and circulate all kinds of memos about helpful, and share all kinds of slogans about what helpful is supposed to be—but none of those things would have anything like the same impact that hearing (and sharing!) that true story would have. Once you've heard that story about Joe and Mrs. Wilson, you know that helpful is not about closing a sale, not about selling products, not about anything that happens to the cash register. It's about people helping people. This is a true story that perfectly captures the essence of the Ace brand promise. And as the store management shares these stories with the employees, it sets the example and shapes the culture.

Make it your goal to create—and share—your own great tribal narrative that supports your company's customer-centric culture!

YOUR AMAZEMENT TOOLBOX

- Past customer service stories can be a great training tool that creates best-practice examples for employees to learn from.

- Your own above-and-beyond stories can demonstrate your core values and help to drive the culture of your company.

- Make it your goal to create and share the next "tribal narrative" that supports your company's customer-centric culture.

THE DRILL

- Think of a time that you created an amazing customer service experience for a customer. (This can be either an internal or an external customer.) What happened?

20

BE A COMMITTED LEARNER

Knowledge is powerful and helps to create trust and confidence.

EARL NIGHTINGALE ONCE POINTED OUT that if we committed ourselves to reading one book a week in a chosen area, each of us could become an authority on that topic. Within five years we could become a national authority. Within seven years we could be an internationally acknowledged expert. Think about that one for a moment!

You can become an authority in *anything you choose* by pursuing your own personal commitment to learning. And guess what? You can do it in a lot less than seven years. Here's my point: The more you know, the more value you can add to others, including (but not limited to) your customers.

Here's the cool part: In our day and age, the knowledge that allows you to add value is ridiculously easy to come across. You can access what you want to know in a traditional book, or in an audio course, or in a video on YouTube, or in any number of other inexpensive or free formats. Yes, you can download an audiobook on virtually any topic of interest, and yes, you can usually finish listening to that audiobook within a week if you choose to make that a priority. But the one thing you can't download is commitment. You have to supply that commodity on your own!

Being a committed learner is all about choosing the field you want to be an expert in, and then leveraging your excitement about that topic to learn everything you possibly can about that field, in partnership with your employer. Being a committed learner is all about being *self-motivated* to improve yourself and raise your own game in an area that excites you. It's all about learning what you love and living what you learn.

Pick your passion! Pick something that connects to your world of work, something you could talk about for hours on end if need be, and never think of as "working." At first, you might not think there are any subjects like that waiting for you in your workplace. I'm here to tell you that if you look hard enough and energetically enough, if you look as part of collaboration with an employer who wants to develop and hold on to good people, *you will find the subject that inspires you.*

Finding that subject, and pursuing it with everything you've got, is a win-win-win. It benefits the customer, it benefits your employer, and it benefits you! Demonstrating knowledge and expertise is a credibility builder—and a career builder too. According to a classic speech from Zig Ziglar, the average American reads fewer than two books a year. Most people don't read purposefully in support of their career. If you do, you will place yourself at a significant career advantage over most of the people in this country.

Make the choice to be a committed learner. Make it a point to learn at least one new thing a day. What you learn may be in an article you come across in a trade publication. Or perhaps you take a few minutes to learn about a product you aren't that familiar with yet. What possibility excites you most? You might sign on for an in-house training session on a new product, a new piece of software, or a general business lesson that's covered during the weekly meeting. Or maybe your company—like Ace—is already deeply committed to continuing education on both the corporate and the store level. Find out what the options are!

Be on the lookout for continuing education programs that are already in place, programs that support both the employee and the company. See what they have to offer. Kramer Ace Hardware, in Mason City, Iowa, for instance, sponsors 20 credit-hours of continuing education per year for full-time associates, and 10 credit-hours per year for part-timers. The subjects are chosen collaboratively by management and the associates. That kind of program is a good start, but it's only a start. Keep the momentum going! Become a committed learner: begin every working day looking for new ways to continue your own personal journey of learning.

YOUR AMAZEMENT TOOLBOX

- You can become an authority on *anything you choose* by pursuing your own personal commitment to reading.

- Demonstrating knowledge and expertise is a credibility builder— and a career builder too.

- Expanding your own knowledge base makes you more valuable to customers and to your employer.

- Begin every working day looking for new ways to continue your own personal journey of learning.

THE DRILL

- How do you plan to continue your own personal development?

21

MENTORING

Get a mentor. Be a mentor.

A MENTOR IS A "wise and trusted counselor or teacher." One of my most important personal aspirations in life is to be a good mentor to others—to help others get and achieve what they want.

This is not a business-oriented goal; it's a goal on the charitable side. I always want to find new ways to help others get what they want from life, to make some kind of inspiring progress on their own journey through life. I want to help people get where they feel they need to go next in their own mission, and I want to do that without getting anything in return from the person other than to know that they have succeeded. I've made this a goal of mine because I have been lucky enough to have several great mentors in my life, including my close friends Bud Dietrich, Kim Tucci, and the late John Ferrara, who were all very helpful when I first started my business.

That's the way it works with mentorship. First you must be mentored, then you must become one.

It didn't surprise me much to learn that mentorship is woven deeply into the culture of Ace Hardware. Shannon Carney, whose family owns Ace stores in Southern California, actually starts the "mentoring process" before the person is hired! A favorite interviewing strategy of Shannon's is to take a promising applicant out onto the floor and to assign an Ace associate to stay close to the potential associate and serve as an instant source of information. Shannon and the mentor watch how the applicant interacts with customers. They are especially looking to see whether this new applicant has what it takes to be helpful! If you have a strong face-to-face interview and do well during the "instant mentorship" exercise, you have a good chance of getting the job.

The mentorship process doesn't stop there, of course. Over the initial weeks and months of any new associate's time with Ace, Shannon makes sure that the new hire is "shadowed" by a mentor associate who can provide guidance, feedback, and support. The "shadow mentor" continues to help the new hire until he or she settles in, feels comfortable with the job, and owns the necessary skill set. The beauty of this system is that it doesn't limit mentorship to the executive ranks. Eventually, everyone in the store can (and should) play the role of mentor. Even if you were just hired a few months ago, you may find yourself "shadowing" a new hire at Ace once you've developed a strong skill set. That makes *you* a mentor!

YOUR AMAZEMENT TOOLBOX

- Once you have been mentored, you have an informal obligation to be a mentor to others.

- Consider an "instant mentorship" during interviews with promising applicants. Watch how they interact with customers.

- Consider a "shadow mentor" program that assigns an experienced employee to guide and support each new hire.

THE DRILL

- Who have been the most important mentors in your life, and why?

- Do you have an example of a time when you taught or mentored someone?

22

STARTING OVER

No matter how great our reputation is for amazing service, we're only as good as our last customer.

ONE OF MY FAVORITE restaurants in my home town of St. Louis is Tony's. It's a local institution, and I couldn't even begin to list all the honors, awards, and accolades it has received for fine dining and fine service over the years. I was talking with owner Vince Bommarito about some of the secrets he's accumulated over the years for delivering great service, and he was kind enough to share one of them with me: A refusal to rest on his laurels.

"We never rest on our reputation," he told me, "because we know we start over with each meal, every night. We earn our reputation anew each time a guest is seated. We treasure the letters we receive from guests from around the world. Our guests are our family. But we don't let their praise fool us into thinking that anything we accomplished yesterday changes what we need to accomplish today."

Just about every day, Vince gets phone calls, emails, and letters offering heartfelt praise about the restaurant, the food, and even specific employees. Every night, just before Tony's opens, he calls an all-employee meeting during which he shares these accolades with the staff by reading the latest expressions of customer love right out loud. There are usually several new pieces of fan mail to read at each of these meetings, and hearing them

116

makes everyone in the room glow. Then Vince tells everyone, "These are great, and we should all be proud. But guess what? In five minutes those doors will open and we start over!"

Then they do!

I was reminded of Tony's ritual when interviewing Ace Hardware's Tom Glenn. He and his family own over a dozen stores in Tennessee. Tom's managers hold team meetings throughout the week during which they share some of the accolades they have received for the great service and help that associates have provided to their customers. The managers also share some of the store's sales numbers. Tom says that giving associates access to this sales information makes them feel closer to the company, and I think he's right. How does he end some of these meetings? With a reminder that gets repeated on a regular basis: "We're only as good as yesterday's numbers."

We all could take a tip from meetings like these. We all could use an ongoing reminder that no matter how good we may think our reputation may be, or how successful we are, we need to earn it all over again with each and every new customer interaction. We're only as good as our last customer and yesterday's numbers. Every day is an opportunity to start over.

YOUR AMAZEMENT TOOLBOX

- No matter how great our reputation for amazing service is, we're only as good as our last customer.

- Share the fan mail and other expressions of love you get from customers, but remember to start from scratch with each new customer.

- Earn your company's reputation for good service, all over again, with each new customer interaction.

- When it comes to delivering amazement, every day is an opportunity to start over.

THE DRILL

- What experiences and lessons from yesterday can you use to deliver amazement today?

- How can you do even better?

CHAPTER EIGHT

ONE-ON-ONE

"Customers perceive service in their own unique, idiosyncratic, emotional, irrational, end-of-the-day, and totally human terms. Perception is all there is!"

—TOM PETERS

I HAVE USED THE term "one-on-one" to describe this interaction in its broadest sense. It can be in person, over the phone, via email, texting, or any other form of direct communication.

It is your direct interaction with your customers, both internal and external, that will ultimately determine your own success and that of your company. Managed well, these interactions will succeed in engaging, amazing, and winning the loyalty of your customers. The next sixteen Amazement Tools (#s 23–38) help you to manage Moments of Truth and create Moments of Magic.

One-on-One Tools

23. It's Showtime!

24. Treat Customers the Way They Want to Be Treated

25. Focus on the Customer, Not the Money

26. Manage the First Impression

27. Engage!

28. Ask the Extra Question

29. One to Say Yes, Two to Say No

30. Cross-Sell and Up-Sell!

31. Last Impressions

32. Be Accountable

33. The Customer Is Not Always Right

34. Bounce Back

35. Master the Art of Recovery

36. Manage the Wait

37. Avoid Loyalty Killers

38. Seize the Moment!

23

IT'S SHOWTIME!

Put on the show of your life, every single time you walk onstage!

AS MENTIONED IN TOOL #14, Shift Your Vocabulary, Disney has very cool terminology for the people who work at its theme parks. If you are employed at one of the Disney properties, you're not known as an "employee." You're a cast member! And the people who pay to visit and enjoy the park? They're your audience! This vocabulary serves to remind everyone that every interaction with every single Guest isn't just a job. It's a performance, and you'd better be ready for your moment in the spotlight when it comes around!

The good people at Ace have learned precisely the same lesson. The minute they step into the store they know they're about to make contact with an "audience." That means they're in a heightened, prepared state of mind—and they're ready to perform. You'll notice the moment you walk into an Ace store that the associates are there to amaze you.

This sense of being ready for the show, ready for prime time, simply means being prepared to engage with customers the moment the "curtain" goes up and they walk into the store. It means embracing the fact that you really do have an audience—in the form of your customer. And it means being committed to please that audience. Here's what Lucinda, an Ace customer in Encinitas, California, had to say about the quality of that performance:

"I am very impressed by this Ace Hardware store. I was in there twice this week, and both times, staff was very helpful. The first time, I was guided through the store as the staff member helped me locate each and every item on my list. The second time, I had questions about drywall repair, and a different staff member gave me lots of helpful advice, which worked beautifully . . . Prices seem to be comparable, yet the service here is light-years ahead."

That's what a great performance looks like. Every day that you show up for work, your goal needs to be the same: to give the performance of your life, to raise the standard of your performance above the one you gave yesterday. That's what showtime is all about! It's a command performance. You leave whatever problems you may be experiencing in the dressing room. You're totally professional. When you show up for your entrance, *you're on*!

A colleague of mine, Mark Sanborn, is an amazing speaker on leadership. He once made a comment to me about how he wanted to be so good for the audience he was speaking to that day that he "cheated" the audience he had spoken to the day before. That comment was brilliant. He actually attributed it to an article about renowned therapist Michele Wiener Davis, who mentioned how she tried to "cheat" yesterday's patient by being better today. Could Mark Sanborn, recognized as one of the top business speakers in the nation, be better than he was the last time every single time he presents to an audience? Having seen Mark in action, I wouldn't bet against him. The point is that he tries to be.

Call it a *Showtime Moment.* It's the moment when you make a personal commitment to raise your own standards, seize the spotlight, and deliver the performance of your life. Give yourself a Showtime Moment every day, right before you hit the stage. That's what can make the difference.

YOUR AMAZEMENT TOOLBOX

- You're in show business, and your customers are your audience!

- Each interaction with a customer isn't just a job, it's a performance. So be ready for your moment in the spotlight!

- Commit to raising your service standards, every single day.

- Seize the spotlight and deliver the performance of your life for every customer every time.

THE DRILL

- What interaction with a customer do you wish you could have videotaped so that you could have shared it with others as a "best practice"?

- What happened that made it so special?

- How could you repeat that great performance, or even improve upon it, next time?

24

TREAT CUSTOMERS THE WAY THEY WANT TO BE TREATED

Approach customers on their own terms—the way they like to be treated.

IN TOOL #10: To Be the Best Place to Buy, Be the Best Place to Work, we covered my twist on the classic Golden Rule, which I turned into the "Employee Golden Rule." Well, here is another twist on this popular "rule."

Many people have said that following the Golden Rule is a great customer service strategy. It seems to make sense to treat people the way you would want to be treated. However, my friend and colleague Dr. Tony Alessandra disagrees. In the world of customer service, he wants us to follow what he calls "The Platinum Rule": *Treat people the way they want to be treated.*

I can illustrate the difference for you very easily. Let's suppose that you're a sociable person, someone who genuinely likes interacting with others and enjoys learning about what's happening in someone else's world—even if you've just met that person. I realize that may not be your first instinct, but for the sake of argument, let's say it is. Let's say that every new individual you meet is exciting, because that person is an opportunity for you to share new experiences and bond.

Well, when you walk into a store, how do you like to be treated? If you're like me, the odds are that you enjoy a little small talk with the salesperson at the counter. That's how *you* want to be treated. Now, let's suppose you have that personality style, and you're working the counter for Ace, and your very first customer of the day is a gentleman who comes across as more of a "just the facts" kind of person. This guy is in a hurry and just wants to get his merchandise and pay for it. He's not interested in small talk. If he has a question, he just wants the answer, period. Nothing else. Certainly no socializing. He might come across as curt, short, and deeply uninterested in how great a time you and your family had at the ballpark last night. That's just his way of interacting with people.

Are you going to treat him the way you want to be treated, and ask him half a dozen questions about his family and friends that he doesn't want to answer? Or are you going to adapt to his style and keep it "all business"?

Obviously, the right thing to do is to adapt to his communication style, his priorities, and his agenda. That's part of your job in the world of customer service. He's not there to adapt to you. You're there to adapt to him!

Without getting into a long dissertation about behavioral styles, let me just say that this responsibility to adapt to the customer is both a personal and an organizational issue. As you'd expect, Ace trains its people in *quickly* adapting to the customer. Ace associates are trained to recognize both the key personality priorities and the key task-driven priorities. Both kinds of priorities are important if you plan to follow the Platinum Rule.

Accordingly, Ace has broken its customer base down into five major subgroups to help associates quickly identify the reason the customer is most likely coming into the store. Different types of customers have different needs. Those subgroups are:

Mission Shoppers: customers who know exactly what they want

Browsers: customers browsing for certain items or pricing

Project Shoppers: customers working on repair, maintenance, and home improvement projects

Business Customers: schools, churches, local businesses, general or subcontractors who buy materials for their business or organization

Service Customers: customers bringing an item in for repair

Someone who's on a mission to replace a single outdoor patio light, for instance, probably has a different set of objectives than someone who's trying to get in-store service on a screen door that their pet cat has scratched to bits. The associates can confirm their initial "diagnosis" about the purpose of the visit with just a few simple questions. Recognizing the objective and adapting to it is just as important as recognizing the communication style and adapting to that. That means you have to pay attention!

Which brings us to a key takeaway here: The more attention you pay to your customers, the better you will be at following the Platinum Rule!

YOUR AMAZEMENT TOOLBOX

- Dr. Tony Alessandra says that to follow the Platinum Rule: Treat people the way THEY want to be treated.

- Customers have different communication styles. Determine how they like to communicate and adapt to that.

- Customers are not there to adapt to the way you like to communicate. You're there to adapt to them!

- Understanding your customers' different buying behaviors allows you to adapt to the way they want to do business.

THE DRILL

- Have you ever had a customer who had a very different expectation of something than you did—or a very different communication style? What was different? Were you able to adapt?

25

FOCUS ON THE CUSTOMER, NOT THE MONEY

The function of your business is not to make money. It is to get and keep customers.

WHAT IS THE FUNCTION of your business? Most of the time, when I ask people this question, I hear this answer: "To make money." But you know what? That really *isn't* the function of your business.

Whenever people tell me that the function of their business is to make money, I ask them to tell me the difference between the function of a business and the goal of a business. Yes, the goal of a business is to make money. (If your organization is a nonprofit, the goal is to fulfill the mission.) But the function of a business is something very different.

Consider these important and wise words from Dr. Theodore Levitt, senior professor at Harvard Business School:

The function of every business and organization
is to get and keep customers.

You can't confuse the function, getting and keeping customers, with the goal. The bottom line is that without customers, you can't make money. This is what leads us to a key best practice at Ace:

Focus on the customer, not the money.

This is an extremely powerful concept.

Do you remember the example I shared with you back in chapter three, when the Ace associate took care of fixing the bike for the cyclist who had been in an accident? That Ace associate was more interested in taking care of the person than he was in making money. Heck, the cyclist wasn't even a customer, only a potential customer! But the outcome was powerful. He became an evangelist for Ace Hardware that day!

You might think this kind of thing is a rare occurrence for Ace, a special kind of incident that headquarters talks about just to win some good PR, but you'd be wrong. In researching this book, I came across dozens of Ace stories like this, situations where Ace employees went WAY above and beyond the call for people who hadn't even bought anything from the store!

The key is to put the customer first. The money follows. This really is how they do business at Ace: They focus on the people, not the money! That's how they get and keep customers.

There were far more of these Good Samaritan stories about Ace than I could possibly have included in this book. I'll share just one more with you so you can get a sense of the powerful loyalty these incidents create in the base of current and prospective Ace customers—and can create in your base of current and prospective customers too.

Maria lives in Mesa, Arizona. Her eight-year-old daughter, Lisa, saw one of those color-changing mood rings in the mall, got her mom to buy it for her, pushed it onto her finger, and fell in love with it. Unfortunately, the ring wouldn't come off. Try as she might, Maria couldn't get the ring off Lisa's finger once they got home, and after an hour of effort, the poor little girl was starting to have some circulation problems.

What did Maria do? She and Lisa hopped in the car and went over to the local Ace Hardware store, where she asked the staff if they had any ideas about how to get the problematic ring off. Floyd, an associate, had an idea. Out came a special pair of pliers, which Floyd maneuvered very carefully to avoid hurting Lisa. After a few minutes of focused attention from all concerned, Lisa's finger was free again.

Maria took a picture of Lisa showing off her newly liberated finger at the Ace store; she was smiling broadly. She posted the photo on Facebook and told everyone exactly what had happened. The post got a great response! "Score one more for the locally owned small business," one person wrote. "Everyone go and give them some love (business)!"

Did Floyd sell anything when he got the ring off Lisa's finger? Nope.

Did he stand out from his competition? Absolutely!

Did he win customers for life, and evangelists? You bet!

Sure, those are extreme examples. Yet every day there are opportunities that, while far less dramatic, put that principle into practice. A customer may be looking for an item that is out of stock. Rather than just send the customer away, the Ace associate may call a competitor and ask them to hold the item for the customer.

Taking it a step further, maybe the associate actually goes to a nearby competitor, buys the item and then comes back to the store, selling it to the customer for the same price he just bought it for. (I heard of more than one instance of this happening at Ace.)

In both of these examples, the customer is more important than the profit. But customers reciprocate with loyalty, and when they do, profit follows.

Put the customer first! Remember that the function of every business is to get and keep customers. The goal is to make money. Confuse the function with the goal, and you don't always reach your goal.

YOUR AMAZEMENT TOOLBOX

- Focus on the customers, not the money!

- Dr. Theodore Levitt said, "The function of every business and organization is to get and keep customers."

- Don't confuse the goal of your business with its function: getting and keeping customers.

- Put your customers first, even before the sale, and they will reciprocate with loyalty.

THE DRILL

- Think of a time when you or a colleague helped a customer even though you didn't make a sale. What did you do, specifically, that made the customer feel that you cared more about him or her as an individual than just another sale?

26

MANAGE THE FIRST IMPRESSION

The first impression sets the tone for whatever is to follow!

IN A RECENT CUSTOMER service survey, 48 percent of respondents said that the most critical time for a company to gain their loyalty was when they make their very first purchase or begin service.[3]

That's a pretty big number! It serves as a powerful reminder that *first impressions count.* Yet everywhere we go as customers, we see evidence that many companies don't seem to care very much about the first impression they make. The customer's initial encounter with those companies is many times a Moment of Mediocrity—average at best—and sometimes even a Moment of Misery.

My take on first impressions is that they are much more than the very first time you meet or decide to do business with someone. First impressions can be the first time or the 500th time you interact with someone. The first impression is any initial interaction you have with someone that sets the tone for whatever is to follow.

This can be the first impression you make when walking into a room. What messages are you sending with your body language or your facial

---

3   "First Impressions Critical for Fueling Customer Loyalty," Marketing Charts, April 16, 2012. www.marketingcharts.com/wp/direct/first-impressions-critical-for-fueling-customer-loyalty-21788/.

expression? Are you dressed for success, which means dressing appropriately for whatever situation you're in? A first impression can be conveyed in the way you answer the phone. Do you welcome someone into the conversation with the words you use and your tone of voice, or do you make the caller feel as if he or she is an interruption? All of those decisions go toward making either a positive or a negative first impression. This is a basic Moment of Truth.

If you've ever been inside an Ace Hardware store, you already know that they're quite good at this first impression tactic. I won't say it's *impossible* to walk into one of these stores without being greeted within ten seconds in a friendly and authentic way, by a real human being who genuinely wants to help you find what you're looking for. It could happen, but not very often. Try it yourself and see.

City after city, store after store, visit after visit, Ace customers notice that they're *greeted* on an individual basis, warmly and helpfully, each and every time they enter the store. Their first impression is that they are made to feel welcome in the store, made to feel as though they've come to the right place. They aren't made to feel like they've broken up a private party. That positive initial greeting—a core best practice—sets the tone for the *helpful* experience Ace aims to deliver to every customer every time.

YOUR AMAZEMENT TOOLBOX

- Manage first impressions. They set the tone for everything that follows!

- The first impression can be the first time you meet or work with a customer or the 500th time.

- Strive to make every customer's first impression a Moment of Magic, every time.

THE DRILL

- What do you do to manage the first impression? How do you greet people? What do you wear to work? Do you shake hands? How do you answer the phone?

- Is there an opportunity for improvement?

27

ENGAGE!

*Use open-ended questions to launch a strong dialogue with
the customer.*

PERHAPS ONE OF THE most asked questions in the world is "How are you?" The standard answer you typically receive is, "Fine," even if the person isn't fine. It's just how most people answer the question. In the retail business, there is a similar question that elicits the same type of automatic, lackluster response. The question sounds like this: "Can I help you?" Of course, the standard response is something like, "No. I'm just looking." Once in a while you'll get a good response from a customer, but usually it's an opportunity for the customer to avoid interacting with a salesperson.

One area in which Ace Hardware flat out excels in its marketplace is in creating and sustaining quality conversations with customers and prospective customers. If you've spent any significant amount of time at a well-run Ace store, you know exactly what I'm talking about. Store after store, you will see the associates interacting with the customer in a way that is comfortable, nonintrusive, and totally appropriate to the individual. People who drop by an Ace store genuinely like talking to the folks who work there. Not every retailer can claim that. In fact, very few can.

How do they do it? There is one powerful universal communication tactic that Ace executes at a world-class level when it comes to engaging with its customers: the tactic of using effective *open-ended questions* to launch and sustain dialogue.

An open-ended question is one that elicits more than a yes-or-no response. Most service providers get the initial exchange with the customer off to a poor start by asking a closed-ended question like, "Can I help you?" Consumers are already in the habit of offering a response like, "No, thanks, I'm just looking." Avoiding a closed-ended question may seem to you like a rudimentary concept, and if it does, you're right. This *is* a very basic tactic, but it is one that is overlooked all the time anyway.

As I mentioned above, Ace excels in creating quality conversations, and they start those conversations with open-ended questions. These questions are delivered with tonality and body language that communicate an authentic interest in the other person. The body language and the tonality take a little practice, but the open-ended structure of the questions Ace associates ask is something that you can master almost instantly. Here are three classic Ace questions you can easily adapt to your world:

- *What can I help you find today?* This question automatically steers the conversation toward the Ace brand promise, helpful, and appeals to one of the most likely reasons a customer is walking into an Ace store in the first place: to solve a single home repair problem or find a single product. You can easily adapt this question to just about any situation; you might ask customers, for instance, what you can help them learn more about, or what prompted them to reach out to you.

- *How are you going to use this?* This query helps the Ace associate determine if there is a larger issue that the customer is really trying to solve. If there's one thing customers like talking about, it's the problem they're facing right now. This question gives the customer an invitation to share all the relevant details.

- *Who is this project for?* If there is more than one decision maker involved in the purchase, this question will usually uncover who it is. That's important information!

Don't make the mistake of assuming that these powerful questions are limited to retail settings. They can cross over to virtually every industry.

They give you the "who, what, when, where, and why" of what the customer is looking for.

An open-ended question that creates engagement should come right after your first impression. (See Tool #26: Manage the First Impression.) You can greet the person and set the tone for what's to follow and then immediately engage with open-ended questions to get information that will help you begin to amaze the customer.

YOUR AMAZEMENT TOOLBOX

- Effective open-ended questions can help you launch and sustain a dialogue with customers and prospective customers.

- Asking customers what you can help them find or learn more about lets you know the reason they are there or have called you.

- Asking customers how they're planning to use what they're looking for gives you additional information you need to help them.

- Asking customers who the project or purchase is for may tell you whether others are involved in the decision-making process.

THE DRILL

- What's the first question you ask a customer to start a conversation and find out what you can do to truly help him or her? (Hint: It's not, "Can I help you?")

- How does that question help you engage with the customer?

28

ASK THE EXTRA QUESTION

Questions are a powerful way to understand expectations, gain clarity, and avoid misunderstandings.

WHAT USUALLY HAPPENS WHEN a customer asks a question?

He or she gets an answer. (The right answer, we hope.)

However, sometimes just getting the right answer to a question isn't enough. That's because sometimes the customer may be asking the wrong question.

For example, a customer may ask for something to be taken care of "quickly." Unless you ask, "How quickly?" you have no idea of what the customer's expectation is. Quickly to him or her may be five or ten minutes. Quickly to you might mean an hour. If the customer's expectation is not identified, and then met, you risk having a Moment of Misery.

So what's the solution? Ask an extra question.

The people at Ace have a best practice that matches up with this principle. It helps them deliver a Moment of Magic virtually every time a customer asks a question. *They know that just answering the question is not enough, so they ask another question of their own.*

This critical best practice is reinforced constantly with frontline service providers—and everyone else, for that matter. It's one of the things you learn to notice about a great service organization: They keep interacting with you after they've done the bare minimum of answering your question.

This actually happened to me at my favorite Ace Hardware, near where I live, in a suburb of St. Louis, Missouri. It happened a few years ago. I was doing a small home repair project, just as most Ace customers do. This particular project involved a small hinge component that had worked its way loose on a swinging, saloon-type door in my home. That little "doohickey" had bent and come right out of the wall, and it needed to be replaced.

I took the broken part over to my local Ace store, showed it to Matt, the young man who had met me at the counter, and asked him whether he could point me toward a replacement part that matched the one I had in my hand.

"I sure can," Matt said. With those words, he had met my basic, minimal expectation. He'd answered my question. The part was in stock. Now if he could just show me where to find it, I'd be a happy man.

Matt did more than that, though. After he took me over to exactly where that replacement part was located in the store, he did something amazing. He continued the conversation by asking an extra question.

Matt said, "Just out of curiosity, what are you using this for?"

To tell you the truth, I hadn't really been expecting that question, because, like a lot of Ace customers, I had just one thing on my to-do list. I wanted to buy that replacement part, return home, fix my door, and move on with the rest of my day. But something about the way he asked made it clear to me that Matt was on my side. He didn't just want me to buy what I wanted. He wanted me to buy what I needed.

So I told him all about my project, about the swinging door, and how the little hinge had worked its way out of the wall. I told him that I was going to screw the new hinge in where the old one had been.

Matt thought for a moment, then said, "Well, you can do it that way, but the problem is, it's going to come right back out again. Maybe a month from now, maybe six months or a year from now, but it will. And when it does, you're going to be right back here again, looking for the same replacement part. There's another way to fix it that will keep your swinging door on its hinges for a lot longer. Can I show it to you?"

Talk about a Moment of Magic! Of course I said yes. Of course I followed Matt's recommendation. And of course any time I have a question about a home repair project, I go back to that Ace store. You know who I'm looking for: Matt! (Actually, though, Matt is one of a half-dozen people in that store who would have had the same kind of helpful conversation with me, with the same outcome.)

What might have happened in another hardware store if I asked, "Do you have this part in stock?" You guessed it. Typically, the counter person would have glanced at the part I'd brought in, looked up at me for a moment, and said something like, "Aisle 19, on the left, three-quarters of the way down." I'd have gotten the right answer to my question, but I would have been left completely on my own. Matt didn't leave me on my own. He continued the conversation. As a result, he saved me a lot of extra work—and won a customer for life.

I love this story, not because it stood out as an exception, but because it perfectly captures what Ace is all about: Helpful. I've shared this story with many people. That's one of the things that happens when you consistently exceed your customers' expectations, by the way: They tell people all about what happened!

YOUR AMAZEMENT TOOLBOX

- Ask the extra question(s). Sometimes a customer says one thing but may mean something else. If you don't ask, you won't know.

- Once you answer a customer's question, continue the conversation. Listen for more information that allows you to give a better answer.

- Some customers think they want one thing, but need something else. Ask questions, listen, and help them understand what they need.

- Ask about the customer's problem and solve it. You could win a customer for life!

THE DRILL

- When have you asked a customer a "follow-up" question that uncovered new information that allowed you to help the customer in a way you would not have done otherwise? (Often, these are questions that begin with words like, "Just out of curiosity . . .")

- If you haven't asked that "extra question," what could you have asked?

29

ONE TO SAY YES, TWO TO SAY NO

Empower your people to come up with a solution.

IT'S EASY TO SAY, "I'm sorry, we don't have that . . . We can't get it . . . We can't do that . . . It's not our policy," and so on. In other words, it's easy to say "No."

But that's not what great companies do. Great companies empower their employees to find solutions for their customers. They teach them to "think outside of the box" for the benefit of the customer. And, they make them feel comfortable enough, if necessary, to find a manager or leader who can help them say "Yes," before they have to say "No."

At Ace, a single associate can't just say "No" without exhausting all options. It takes two people to say "No," and one person to say "Yes." A "No" requires approval from the manager!

This approach has been around for a long time, but I had never seen it in action. After discussing it in one of my interviews with Jay Heubner, Ace's Director of Retail Training, I started noticing that other companies were embracing the approach, and even calling it the same thing.

This may be the ultimate expression of a customer-centric philosophy. You're asking the employee to figure out how to get or give the customer what they want or need. Suddenly, the employee is all about solving your customer's problems, not getting out of the conversation. A nice by-product of this practice is that it cuts down on employees having to "get a manager's approval."

The story about Josh in Tool #11: Don't Take the Easy Way Out, is an excellent example. That was where the customer, Judy, called to buy a lawnmower that the store didn't stock. Josh, the associate, didn't have to go to his manager to ask if it was okay to call the Toro dealer. To him it was common sense to make the call, which turned into a sale.

There is another by-product, and this is huge. When an employee feels he or she has to say "No" to the customer, the manager may be able to show them how to say "Yes." That becomes a real-time learning experience that the employee will be able to use the next time he or she encounters a similar situation.

You want to have a culture that *never* takes the easy way out and has the amazing customer-centric mindset against automatically telling a customer *No*.

YOUR AMAZEMENT TOOLBOX

- The goal is to say YES! Create a culture that makes it mandatory for TWO people to sign off on any denial of a customer request.

- It's easy to say "No" to a customer, but that's not what amazing companies do. They find ways to say "Yes."

- *One to say yes and two to say no* is an empowerment strategy. Train employees to provide solutions on their own!

- When employees seek out a manager to get approval, it should be a teaching experience, with no approval needed next time.

THE DRILL

- Can you think of a time when it would have been much easier to say "No" to a customer, but you found a way instead to say "Yes"?

- How did you feel?

- How do you think the customer felt?

30

CROSS-SELL AND UP-SELL!

Trust makes all the difference.

CROSS-SELLING IS WHAT YOU DO when you suggest that a customer who's already buying something from you buy something else from another department. Up-selling is when you suggest that a customer buy something related to what they are already buying from you. In both cases, you are asking the customer to buy something they hadn't thought to buy.

For example, if you have a checking account at a bank, the teller may suggest that you see someone in the residential mortgage department in the offices next door who can help you secure a home loan. (That's a cross-sell.)

Or, you might be at a nice restaurant and the server suggests an appetizer that the restaurant is well known for. You weren't planning to order the appetizer, but the server convinces you to do so. (That's an up-sell.)

In both cases, there is the opportunity to grow the bottom line of a business, but more importantly, these are opportunities to create a better experience for the customer. And, here's the most important part: If they know they could create a better experience for the customer, and they don't do it, they are doing the customer a disservice.

Most people think that the cross-sell or up-sell is just more selling. Even though the word "selling" is here, it really isn't selling. It's servicing.

That said, there are definitely some people who may be better at it than others. You can have a training class on this, and I'm sure that because of that word "selling," it may appear to be sales training. However, if you think about this in terms of amazing your customer, you will find that it takes on a different look.

If you go to your local Ace Hardware store to buy paint, and the sales associate doesn't ask you if you need brushes or a drop cloth, that sales associate is doing you a disservice. One of the most powerful strategies Ace uses is to make sure that if you come in for a project, you leave with everything you need, so you don't have to make extra trips to Ace or any other store. That may include recommending items you didn't know you needed. There's nothing high-pressure or "sales-y" about recommendations like that. That's just one neighbor helping another neighbor.

Ace associates learn two critical principles when it comes to cross-selling and up-selling. First, they should only recommend that a customer purchase something else from them when they are 100 percent certain that it is the right thing to do. If they ever make a recommendation that violates that principle, they'll destroy the trust they've built up with the consumer. Second, if they know for sure that buying a certain product will save a customer a headache, or another trip out to the store, they *must* recommend the purchase. It's a dereliction of duty not to!

Regardless of your business, if you don't ask questions or make suggestions that will enhance the customer's experience by leveraging your products and or services, you are missing a great opportunity for amazement.

YOUR AMAZEMENT TOOLBOX

- To not cross-sell or up-sell your customers is doing them a disservice. Done right, this is not sales. It's customer service.

- Only recommend that a customer purchase something else when you are 100 percent certain it is the right thing to do.

- If you notice a purchase that you know would help the customer, and you don't recommend it, you have failed the customer.

THE DRILL

- Think of a time when a customer was thinking about purchasing one thing, and you made a "cross-sell or up-sell" recommendation that helped the customer to do and accomplish more by buying more. What would have happened if you had not made the recommendation? Would the customer have been better off or worse off?

31

LAST IMPRESSIONS

Leave a great lasting impression!

THIS IS ONE OF THOSE critical Moments of Truth that is all too easy to overlook.

Earlier in this section (Tool #26: Manage the First Impression) we covered delivering a positive first impression, and how it is extremely important in terms of our overall engagement strategy with the customer. Just as important, if not even more so, is the *last* impression—because that's what will leave the *lasting* impression.

If we make sure the customer's last experience during the service encounter is a positive one—an above-average experience, an amazing experience—then the customer will self-reinforce that positive emotion on our behalf for a long, long time after the actual transaction. Maybe that positive reinforcement will express itself during the ride home when the customer thinks about how nice it was to have someone who smiled, who listened, who helped the way we did during the last few moments the customer was with us.

Maybe it's as simple as the positive "Goodbye, and have a great day!" that comes at the end of a phone call that makes the customer feel that the company appreciates his or her business. Or maybe, right after an online purchase, the customer who's concerned about whether or not everything processed correctly while placing the order finds an email message from us almost instantly after hitting the "Confirm Purchase" button. That email tells her that her order has been placed, that everything is in order, and that she doesn't need to do anything else. Based on that one timely email, she congratulates herself for picking the right online store to order from. That's the power of the last impression!

These are the kinds of consumer perceptions that advertising agencies get paid millions of dollars to shape. We can shape them for a lot less with something as simple as a smile, or an offer to help the customer on the way out of the store, or a personalized follow-up via email.

One of the things you notice immediately about shopping at Ace Hardware is that the associates who work there are often very concerned about helping you get your purchase into your car, helping you load whatever it is you've bought into your trunk or backseat. That's no accident. They're trained to do that, and it only takes a few minutes searching customer reviews online to figure out that people like this aspect of shopping at Ace—a lot!

Does it take a little more time and effort to help the customer load up the car? Sure. But Ace has made the shrewd strategic decision that making that investment makes all the sense in the world. Leaving the customer with a positive last impression does three important things. First, it helps to overcome any service missteps that may have been made along the way, which is an important consideration when the customer is interacting with multiple people. Second, it gives us the chance to continue the one-on-one conversation with the customer in the parking lot (or wherever), and more interaction is better than less interaction. Third, it gives the customer a reason to think good thoughts about us on the drive back home!

By the same token, a *botched* last impression can undo everything positive that has happened to the consumer up to that point! All that the customer will remember is the scowl and the refusal she got when she asked for help loading a big box into the car. That Moment of Misery really can erode all of the positive interactions encountered during the visit.

The *last impression* is a powerful tactic that too many people and companies overlook. Anything less than a strong last impression is simply . . . *not* amazing!

YOUR AMAZEMENT TOOLBOX

- First impressions are important, but the last impression we leave with the customer will leave the most *lasting* impression.

- A strong last impression can help overcome any service missteps that may have been made along the way.

- A positive last impression gives the customer a reason to think good thoughts about us on the drive back home!

THE DRILL

- What do you say or do to ensure that your last impression with the customer is a positive one?

32

BE ACCOUNTABLE

Assume full ownership of the customer's experience.

ACCOUNTABILITY IS A HIGHER LEVEL of being reliable and dependable. It means we take deep personal responsibility for what we do for our customers. It means we take credit for all of the good and accept responsibility for any of the bad. When we are accountable, we assume that *nothing* should stand between our customers and complete satisfaction, and we start considering ourselves personally responsible, not just for meeting their expectations (that's a given), but for exceeding them. How do we do that? By assuming full *ownership* of the customer's experience. As a result of that personal ownership, a very strong bond develops between us and our customers.

Accountable people hold much longer relationships with their customers than people who aren't accountable do; that's because the trust in the relationship reaches an extraordinary level. The customers come to feel that it would be difficult or impossible to find someone who cared as much, or delivered as much, or went above and beyond the call as often.

As Bert, an Ace customer in Seattle, wrote:

> *If you wanted to build and decorate your own unicorn, the unbelievably helpful and knowledgeable people working at this store would be able to cheerfully assist you in the process.*

I'm not kidding. They'd all be like, "Well, first you're going to need to know if you want to make a pneumatic unicorn or a hydraulic unicorn. I can tell you the pros and cons of each, and then send you over to the paint department where Jane will help you choose which sparkly color to use for the horn. You'll want to consider an outdoor, weatherproof paint for that." Then the guy would collect all the pieces of your project, package them neatly, and meet you at the front register with helpful pamphlets called "The Plus Side of Rechargeable Unicorns" and "Weaving Realistic Unicorn Fur by Hand."

Then, I suppose, the guy from Ace calls back a week later to check in and see how the unicorn project is going! Now that's accountability! The customer obviously made up this example to make his point. It's also obvious, though, that he had had the experience of having someone at Ace assume full *ownership* of his experience in the store.

Here's another example. I once told the front-desk clerk at a hotel that my nightstand light was burnt out. She said, "I'll take care of it." Now, that doesn't mean she went up to my room and changed the bulb. No, she called the maintenance department to report the problem. Then she called them back an hour later to make sure the bulb was changed. When she saw me walk by later that evening she told me, "I took care of the burnt-out bulb in your nightstand lamp. And, if you have any other problems, don't hesitate to call me. I'm on duty until midnight, and if I'm not here, any one of my colleagues can help you." That's ownership!

The point is that it's not just the follow-through that should be *amazing*. It's also the follow-*up*. You do what is expected and then follow up to make sure everything has been done right and the customer is happy.

Most companies would be content if their customers thought of them as reliable and dependable. They should be shooting for something higher: accountability. Accountability raises the bar. It means you own the customer's experience. In turn, the customer enjoys this stronger relationship and reciprocates with repeat business, long-term loyalty, and evangelism.

YOUR AMAZEMENT TOOLBOX

- Accountability is a higher level of being reliable and dependable.

- When we are accountable, we assume full *ownership* of the customer's experience.

- When we are accountable, a very strong bond develops between us and our customers.

- Accountability is follow-through and follow-*up*. Do what is expected. Then check in to make sure the customer is happy.

THE DRILL

- Can you think of a time when you assumed personal ownership of solving a problem for a customer?

- Did you follow up to make sure the issue was resolved to the customer's complete satisfaction? What was the customer's response?

33

THE CUSTOMER IS NOT ALWAYS RIGHT

If the customer is wrong, let him be wrong with dignity. After all, he is still the customer!

THERE'S A POPULAR PIECE of bad customer service "advice" I cannot rebut often enough, and will always take the opportunity to do so. No matter what you may have heard to the contrary, *the customer is NOT always right.*

As people who live in the real world, and who have to deal with other people in that real world, we need to accept that it just doesn't do us or our customers any good to pretend that they never make mistakes. They do. Acting like they couldn't ever be wrong usually makes everyone's job harder and more stressful, *however . . .*

What we *do* need to accept is that, *even when a customer is wrong, that person is still the customer, and still deserves to be treated with respect!*

A lot of frontline service people get stressed during exchanges in which they know the customer is wrong, and some even emotionally escalate the exchange in an attempt to settle the matter once and for all. They usually do—by losing the customer!

Mavis Knowles, an Ace manager in Dallas Bay, Tennessee, shared a great story that illustrates exactly the right way to respond when you know or strongly suspect that a customer is wrong. Mavis was getting ready to go on her lunch break when Frank, one of her customers, made his way up to the counter and told her that he had a problem: Ace had recently rescreened one of his daughter's aluminum-frame screen windows and, in the process, had stretched it out of shape.

Now, you don't have to be an expert in window rescreening to know that this complaint of Frank's was not very plausible. You don't bend or reshape the frame in any way when you replace the screen in a removable window. But Frank was insistent: Ace had damaged the window. It no longer fit where it was supposed to fit.

Frank had the window screen with him. Mavis looked it over. It showed no signs of damage at all.

It's at this point that a lot of frontline service providers might have made the mistake of getting into an argument about who was right and who was wrong. Mavis could have done that. She could have said, "I'm sorry, Frank, I'm about to go on my lunch hour, and you can talk to someone else here about this if you want, but I can guarantee you that nothing we did while rescreening this window changed its shape in any way."

She could have said that. But she didn't. What Mavis said was, "Well, I'm leaving for lunch now, anyway. How far away are you? Maybe we can take a look at what the problem is."

Wow!

Frank's daughter's house was only a block away. So Mavis followed him over there. When she got to the room where Frank was having the problem, she noticed that as he tried to insert the screen, he was trying to force it into the *upper* part of the window, which was not where it belonged. She asked if she could give it a try. Frank said, "Sure."

Mavis easily slid the screen window into the *lower* compartment, where it fit perfectly! She had solved the problem—and won a customer for life.

Maybe you're not ready or willing to make on-site inspections of your customer's possible error points, as Mavis was. But you *should* be ready and willing to treat the customer with respect, give him or her the benefit of the doubt, and avoid escalating the discussion into a debate or an argument over who's "right." No matter who "wins" that conversation, you will lose!

It can't be said often enough: The customer is NOT always right, but they are always the customer. So, if they are wrong, let them be wrong with dignity and respect.

YOUR AMAZEMENT TOOLBOX

- Even when customers are wrong, you still have to treat them with respect. After all, they are your customers!

- If you know or strongly suspect that a customer is in error, avoid escalating into an argument over who's right.

- Give customers who are wrong the benefit of the doubt until you can identify what the problem really is.

- The customer is NOT always right, but he or she is always the customer. So, if customers are wrong, let them be wrong with dignity.

THE DRILL

- Can you think of a time when you knew that the customer was not right? How did you respond? How did that make the customer feel?

- Are there any common mistakes your customers make? If so, how do you respond in a way that lets them be wrong with dignity and respect?

34

BOUNCE BACK

No one promised customer service was always going to be easy.
Learn to bounce back!

EVERY ONCE IN A WHILE we're going to find ourselves in a conversation with a customer that takes an unexpected wrong turn, despite our very best efforts. Or maybe we just hit a "bump in the road," for whatever reason, and we know that the service we just provided was not particularly amazing. The bottom line is the customer is upset, even angry.

It happens.

And when it does, our job is actually pretty simple: Bounce Back.

There's a four-step process for Bouncing Back from even a major lapse in communication that leads to a failure to amaze your customer. Here it is:

Step one: Disengage. You know when an exchange with a customer is going nowhere. If it's still possible, try to hand the troublesome discussion off to someone else on your team before it deteriorates any further. If you can't transfer the discussion over to someone else, apologize to the customer (even if—especially if—you think you're "in the right") and ask for a time-out. Get the appropriate contact info. Assure the customer that you or someone else will circle back at a specific time to address the customer's issue. DO NOT engage in an argument about who's "right." Separate yourself from this conversation.

Step two: Cool off. Take some time away from the situation. You've just given yourself a little distance. Make the most of it. Take a break. Don't mentally replay the whole drama you just left. Do something else.

Step three: Learn from what happened. Once you've had time to decompress, ask yourself: How would you do things differently with this customer if you had it to do all over again? Would you begin the conversation differently? Offer a different set of possible solutions to the consumer? Ask a different question?

Step four: Share what you learned. Tell your boss. Tell your colleagues. Make some notes. Use what you've learned about the experience to make your company's process more customer focused. If you use your difficult experience to help create a stronger set of processes for your customer, then everybody wins. As Ace's John Surane, Senior Vice President, Merchandising, Advertising, Marketing and Paint, put it, "What we do on a day-in and day-out basis is bigger than any one experience." What he meant was that the day-to-day process, the accumulated system of best practices that Ace has built up over decades, is strong enough to allow the store to bounce back even when the individual has an "oops" moment.

For example, Samantha, an Ace customer in Healdsburg, California, asked the Ace associate she saw at the front counter where she could find the patio section—and didn't get an amazing response. Whoever was manning the counter that day apparently had an "oops" moment. This is rare—Ace is usually very good at getting customers where they need to go—but it does happen. Once Samantha finally did make her way over to Patio, though, she ran into another Ace associate. This one was "friendly" and "helpful" (Samantha's words, not mine), and she showed Samantha a few things that would go along well with the product she was there to buy. According to Samantha, "There was no pressure to buy anything, and the information she gave me was very valuable." Result? The system worked. As Surane suggested, the processes the store associates were used to executing, and improving, on a daily basis proved to be more important than a single employee's "oops" moment!

Some important points to remember:

Contrary to popular belief, as we discussed in the last tool, the customer is *not* always right, but the customer is always the customer. So as we learned, let him or her be wrong with dignity.

Sometimes, of course, there is a problem, and the customer is right. When that happens, it's time to go into recovery mode. (See Tool #35: Master the Art of Recovery.) Let the customer vent, assure him or her you are there to help, and realize that your job is not just to fix the problem but to restore the customer's confidence.

No matter how contentious your conversation might get, remember that you are not trying to win an argument. You are trying to win the customer!

YOUR AMAZEMENT TOOLBOX

- Contentious exchanges with customers happen. Sometimes it's best to step back, disengage, cool down—maybe even get some help.

- Whenever there is a potentially negative experience with a customer, learn from what happened, and improve the process.

THE DRILL

- Can you think of a time when you had an interaction with a customer that made you upset or even angry? How did you handle it?

- What did you learn from the experience? What would you do differently if the same thing happened again?

35

MASTER THE ART OF RECOVERY

A good recovery is the key to successfully handling complaints.

PART OF CREATING LOYAL CUSTOMERS is how you respond in "recovery mode" when there are problems or complaints. When a customer complains, how do you handle it? Do you work at getting him or her to come back the next time? Or do you get into a discussion—or worse, an argument, about whose fault it is?

A Moment of Misery—and we all have them—is really an opportunity disguised as a problem or complaint. It's a chance to demonstrate your company's "best practices" in the sometimes neglected art of customer service recovery. Those best practices can be adapted to all kinds of different situations in all kinds of different industries, but at the end of the day they always boil down to four basics:

1. Apologize.

2. Take action with an acceptable temporary solution.

3. Make a promise to the customer to resolve the problem.

4. And, finally, keep the promise.

These strategies may sound simple. They may even sound like common sense. Yet, the execution may not always be so simple, and the common sense may not always be so common. Some problems may take a long time to resolve; others can be fixed immediately. Regardless of what the problem is, the end result has to be more than just a fixed problem. It is about restoring confidence. You want the customer to say this: "I love doing business with them. Even when there is a problem, I can count on them."

Eric, an associate at an Ace store in San Jose, California, got a call from a customer who had purchased a can of expensive interior household paint from the store and was in the middle of painting his son's room. The problem was, the paint that was going up on the walls was extremely watery, and it left long drips that looked terrible. The customer had expected better. What could the store do about it?

Step One: Eric immediately apologized for the customer's problem.

Step Two: He thanked the customer for calling. He asked if it would be all right if he, Eric, called the manufacturer directly, and then called the customer back with an update.

Step Three: Before he hung up, he promised to find a way to fix the problem. Notice that Eric saved the customer the time and trouble of calling the manufacturer, waiting on hold, re-explaining his problem, and so on.

Step Four: Eric then phoned back and explained that he had arranged for a free replacement can of paint from the manufacturer, and he apologized again for the problem. He suggested that the customer come by the store and pick up the paint. When the customer showed up, Eric met him personally, apologized once again for the problem, and made sure that the customer got the new can of paint, mixed to the proper color.

That's an absolutely perfect recovery. The Moment of Misery became a Moment of Magic. It stands out because *that's not what usually happens when a customer makes a complaint!* How easy would it have been for Eric to say, "You're going to need to call the manufacturer"? How easy would it have been for him to imply that the customer must have been applying the paint incorrectly? He didn't do any of that—because Ace trains its people in the art of recovery!

In an online review describing this event, the customer gave that Ace store four stars and wrote: "Sometimes, it isn't what goes right that makes a rating, but how a business handles a situation when something goes wrong."

Whenever there is a problem or complaint, what customers really want is the problem fixed, with the right attitude and with a sense of urgency. Follow the four steps in this chapter and you will not only fix the problem but you will also restore their confidence.

Remember: Service recovery is more than just fixing a problem. It's also about the renewal of customer confidence!

YOUR AMAZEMENT TOOLBOX

- A Moment of Misery is really an opportunity disguised as a complaint or problem.

- The basics of service recovery are to apologize, take action, make a promise to resolve the problem, and keep the promise.

- Customers want their problem fixed by someone with a good attitude and a sense of urgency.

- Service recovery is more than just fixing the problem. It's also about renewing customer confidence.

THE DRILL

- Think of a time that a customer complained to you about something and you were able to turn the complaint into a positive experience—one that renewed the customer's confidence. How did you do that?

36

MANAGE THE WAIT

Customers hate to wait. Their time is valuable, so manage the wait . . . and don't be late.

I HAVE A NEW DOCTOR, David Katzman, MD. I switched to Dr. Katzman about two or three years ago. I like going to him for two reasons. First, he is a great doctor. Second, he doesn't make me wait.

When was the last time you went to your doctor's office and the doctor was on time?

I don't know about you, but for me, waiting around at the doctor's office was a pretty typical occurrence until I switched over to Dr. Katzman. My former doctor was notoriously late. I once showed up for what I had been told was the first appointment of the day and discovered that three other patients also had the first appointment of the day!

Sure, *sometimes* that kind of problem happens, but for me it was representative of that doctor's level of respect for his patients' time. We come in a few minutes early, and we wait around for a long time reading magazines. Finally, the receptionist calls our name, and we get excited. We think the doctor is finally going to see us. And what happens? They put us in a room and tell us the doctor will be with us "in a few minutes." Now, I think of "a few" as between three and five. Somehow those "few minutes" turn into 10, 15, maybe even 20 minutes. We start wondering if anybody remembers putting us in the room at all.

It's unfortunate that some "service providers" make the mistake of *over-promising and under-delivering* in terms of customer wait times. That sends customers the wrong message, namely, "My time is more important than yours." Customers hate that. What we ought to be doing is *under-promising and over-delivering.*

For my part, I really, really hate to make clients wait. Whether they are waiting for a product, service, a return phone call, or anything else, it doesn't matter. I know my clients don't like to wait, but I also know that, as a practical matter, sometimes they just have to. So if I have to make them wait, I do my level best to manage the wait. I always try to under-promise and over-deliver when it comes to wait times. I tell customers how long it will be, which creates an expectation, and then I find ways to exceed that expectation. By the way—and this is very important—whenever you create the expectation, you have to do your best to make sure it is one that the customer agrees with and is happy with.

The Disney people are experts at managing the wait. At most Disney theme parks, there are lines, and they are usually long. There is usually a Disney cast member (that's what Disney call its employees) standing at the end of the line helping to direct the line traffic. When you ask the cast member how long the wait is, you get an estimate. When you finally do get to the front of the line, you usually notice that it wasn't quite as long as you were told. If the cast member told you 15 minutes, it probably only took 10 or 12 minutes. You think, "Wow! These guys are good." But, it's not an accident or a one-time occurrence. Disney does it consistently, on purpose. They make an art of this concept!

Ace is an expert at managing the wait too. If you bring in a screen door to Cherry Creek Ace Hardware in Denver, Colorado, and they take on the job of fixing it, they'll usually give you an estimate of how long it will take. When the associate calls the customer sooner than expected, the store comes across as a hero, and so does the associate. You've been amazed! As one Cherry Creek customer posted in an online review, "I love a business that respects the value of my time, and that's a big reason why this place is at the top of my list."

YOUR AMAZEMENT TOOLBOX

- Over-promising and under-delivering, in terms of wait times, gives the customer a reason to want to try the competition.

- If you have to make a customer wait, let the person know how long. Then don't just meet the expectation, exceed it!

- If customers perceive that the wait is *shorter* than they expect, they will praise you—or criticize you for the opposite.

THE DRILL

- Have you ever been able to exceed a customer's expectations in terms of how long he or she had to wait for something? Was it an accident, or did you truly *under-promise and over-deliver*?

- How did the customer react?

37

AVOID LOYALTY KILLERS

Be careful to avoid words and phrases that destroy your customers' confidence and loyalty.

SO FAR WE'VE FOCUSED our attention on "best practices"—strategies that you and your organization should make a point of doing. The guidance you will find in this chapter is how to avoid a few common "worst practices" that some people and companies do that destroy any semblance of a relationship they have with their customers.

There are some Moments of Misery that are so common and create such automatic feelings of ill will with your customers that they automatically start thinking about wanting to do business somewhere else. These Moments of Misery are *Loyalty Killers*, and they are to be avoided at all costs.

The three phrases examined below are the ones that customers flat-out hate hearing, and they'll do just about anything to avoid hearing again, including never doing business with us again. So we definitely DO NOT want to say anything remotely resembling the three phrases I'm about to share! They are the customer service equivalent of plutonium: toxic, dangerous, and deadly. Keep a safe distance from them.

A side note: One of the big reasons I began considering Ace Hardware as the central role model for this book was that I realized it had somehow "operationalized" a culture that (at least in my experience) *did not deliver any of these "Loyalty Killer" moments*. That's a sign of a powerful, positive, employee-centric, customer-centric culture.

Loyalty Killer No. 1: "It's not my department." Customers absolutely loathe this one. Yes, it may not be your department—or your table at a restaurant, or your whatever else—but no, that does not mean you don't have responsibility to take care of this customer. You may not be the one who comes up with the answer or resolves the problem, but you can help customers get *closer* to what they want. Instead of firing off this nuclear Loyalty Killer, you want to find out what the customer's problem is. Once you do, offer to get back to him or her with an answer.

Perhaps you do end up handing off the problem to someone else, but you still stay in the customer's orbit until you are absolutely sure that he or she really is going to be taken care of. (See Tool #32: Be Accountable.)

Loyalty Killer No. 2: "It's against company policy." Or, another way of saying it, "I'm not authorized to do that." Great service lies in flexibility. This Loyalty Killer is the exact opposite of that value, and is a sign of a major cultural problem.

The companies that provide the very best service tend to think in terms of the customer, not in terms of a rulebook. In Tool #13: Defend the Culture, I pointed out that there's a big difference between an *operations-centric* culture and a *customer-centric* culture.

In the first kind of culture, people don't have the flexibility necessary to make intelligent judgment calls on behalf of the customer, even if they want to. In the second kind of culture, they *do* have that flexibility. The kind of culture where management doesn't trust employees to make good decisions on their own isn't customer-centric. In fact, that kind of organizational structure may punish people who try to create intelligent, flexible solutions that don't happen to show up in the "policy manual." The job description may say Customer Service, and there may be all kinds of service-oriented posters on the wall, but in reality, all the employee has to work with is the rulebook. That's not enough.

I think one reason a lot of companies have a problem with flexibility is that they don't trust their employees, and vice versa. Guess what? If the internal culture is all about following rules, then the external customer experience is going to be all about following rules. Ouch! Some companies create rules. Others create guidelines. Guidelines provide for flexibility.

Avoid using the language of "rules and regulations" in your interactions with the customer! Customers don't want to hear about the rulebook. If you have to explain a decision to a customer, do it as a peer. Frame it in terms of the most *helpful* outcome, not in terms of what you are and aren't allowed to do.

Loyalty Killer No. 3: "You need to talk to (whomever). He/she is on vacation (or out for the day, or at a meeting, or whatever) and won't be back until next week." How do YOU feel when some service person says this to YOU? While the statement may be factually accurate, the customer still hates hearing it. Customers don't care what your company's work schedule is, and they don't like "explanations" that leave them without the solution they seek.

Whenever this kind of situation arises, take ownership of the situation. This may mean getting the message to the right person, and then getting back to the customer. Inform the customer about when he or she will get his or her answer. Again, if someone else is doing the follow-up, check in and make sure the customer really *was* taken care of. This may mean making an extra call or two, but so what? Those are precious touch points that let the customer know you care and are on the lookout for ways to help. Your attitude in responding to this situation will go a long way toward creating some goodwill in what could be a negative situation. Take that Moment of Misery and turn it into a Moment of Magic!

YOUR AMAZEMENT TOOLBOX

- Telling a customer, "It's not my department," is a Loyalty Killer.

- You may not come up with the answer or resolve the problem, but you can help customers get *closer* to what they want.

- Telling a customer, "It's against company policy," is a Loyalty Killer.

- Great service lies in flexibility. Rules should be guidelines.

- The companies that provide the very best service tend to think in terms of the customer, not in terms of a rulebook.

- Some companies create rules. Others create guidelines. Guidelines provide for flexibility.

- Telling a customer, "You need to talk to (name) and (he/she) isn't here, so try again later," is a Loyalty Killer.

- Take ownership of getting a customer request to the right person. Follow up to make sure the customer was taken care of.

THE DRILL

- Have you ever been on the receiving end of a "Loyalty Killer" phrase such as "That's not my department" or "Sorry, it's company policy"? If so, how did that make you feel? If not, how do you think you would have felt?

38

SEIZE THE MOMENT!

Every interaction with a customer is an opportunity to show how good you are.

IN CHAPTER FIVE, "The Seven Amazement Principles," I summarized Jan Carlzon's definition of the Moment of Truth:

> Any time a customer comes into contact with any
> aspect of your business, however remote, they have
> an opportunity to form an impression.

That Moment of Truth is virtually every part of the interaction an internal or external customer has with you, from the first moment you engage until the very end of the interaction. At any point along the way, you are creating one of the three Moments of Truth described in chapter five, a negative Moment of Misery, an average Moment of Mediocrity, or (you hope) a positive Moment of Magic. By now you realize that it is your job to seize every moment you have with a customer and turn it into a Moment of Magic. But how do you *know* you are doing it?

Think about simple words customers would use to describe how we interacted with them when we deliver a Moment of Magic. Those words could be: courteous, kind, friendly, nice, neighborly, genuine, and of course, helpful. We can't leave out amazing, either!

These, and similar words, can describe a Moment of Magic. You must seize the moment and deliver on one or more of these descriptive words. For example, a customer in California posted this about the service he received at the Ace store in Palo Alto: "It's the rare feeling of genuine friendliness that makes the place stand out."

Isn't that a review we would all enjoy receiving? We should aspire to deliver a feeling of genuine *friendliness.*

Seizing the moment means never allowing yourself to go on autopilot while you're interacting with a customer. It means learning to ask yourself a critical "self-check" question about every single Moment of Truth that you share with a customer. It means that, at every stage of the interaction, you are fully present in the moment, and self-aware enough to evaluate that moment honestly. You do that by asking yourself this question: Is what I'm doing right now going to make this customer want to come back the next time he or she needs what we sell?

The result of a team member who consistently seizes the moment is an exchange that the customer perceives as *genuinely friendly, helpful, kind, neighborly, and any other words similar to the ones listed above.* This seize the moment strategy, in fact, is one of the most important tools for operationalizing helpful in any organization. It takes practice, though, because for most of us it's a lot easier than it probably ought to be to go on autopilot during an interaction with a customer.

There should be a sign in the break room, a laminated card in the employees' pocket, a plaque on the wall for all, including our customers, to see that reads:

Is what I'm doing right now going to make
this customer want to come back the next time?

YOUR AMAZEMENT TOOLBOX

- What simple words, like "friendly" and "helpful," would customers use to describe the interactions they have with you?

- In every interaction with the customer, be fully present in the moment and self-aware enough to evaluate that moment honestly.

- Ask: Is what I'm doing *right now* going to make this customer want to come back the next time he or she needs what we sell?

THE DRILL

- Think of a time when you delivered an above-average experience to a loyal customer. What, specifically, did you do that made that customer want to come back the next time he or she needed what you sell?

CHAPTER NINE

THE COMPETITIVE EDGE

"If you do build a great experience, customers tell each other about that. Word of mouth is very powerful."

—JEFF BEZOS, CEO OF AMAZON.COM

IF YOU'VE ALREADY CREATED a customer-first culture within your organization, and if you have consistently executed on that culture, then you're ready for the next step.

The next step is simply this: delivering Moments of Magic that go beyond being above average. These moments are the kind that really stand out, the kind that make your customers say "Wow!" The next ten Amazement Tools (#s 39–48) show you how to deliver a customer experience so powerful that it builds intense loyalty, increases evangelism for your brand, and leaves the competition shaking its collective head.

In this chapter, you will find the tools that will help your enterprise to get closer to joining the ranks of the "superstar" service providers!

Competitive Edge Tools

39. Own Your Mile

40. Satisfaction Is a Rating, Loyalty Is an Emotion

41. Be Easy to Do Business With

42. Get Firsthand Experience

OWN YOUR MILE

Do you stand out in your customer community—in an area where you've chosen to excel?

"OWNING YOUR MILE" means finding your niche. It comes from a retail concept—the idea that your store, whatever it sells, should have the best service, the strongest customer loyalty, and the most established presence for any store of its kind within a one-mile radius. Your customers should consider you to be the first place to stop whenever they need whatever it is you sell. This "own your mile" concept, though, definitely isn't just limited to the world of retailing. It is a strategy that works for virtually every type of business!

The *mile* is more than a distance. Owning your mile means standing out within your customer community, in an area where you've chosen to excel. Every company has a "mile" that it should own, a targeted community where it should strive to predominate.

That community may or may not be defined geographically. For Ace, it is the geographical distance around the hardware store itself. And, it may be 1 mile or 10 miles—or more. You can bet that the owner of a successful Ace store knows that *mile* inside and out!

For you and your company, it might be five miles or a whole city or a global community of people interested in what you sell. For example, my mile is helping companies with their customer service. My geographical area may be the world. My focused community is anyone interested in delivering a better customer experience. I want to *own* that mile. When you think of customer service, I want you to think of me.

Know what your mile looks like, sounds like, and acts like. Is it a certain region? Is it a particular demographic? Is it a particular subject or topic, as in my case? For an Ace store, owning the mile means embodying helpful for each and every person in that store's community—specifically, those who have a home improvement project, a maintenance issue, need something for their garden, a repair, etc. If you happen to fall into that category, and you have the good fortune to walk into an Ace Hardware store when you need help, you can find out for yourself just how much the people in that store are willing to do in order to own their mile and amaze you each and every time you show up.

YOUR AMAZEMENT TOOLBOX

- "Owning your mile" means standing out in your customer community, in any area where you've chosen to excel.

- Every company has a "mile" that it should own, a targeted community where it should strive to predominate.

- Owning a mile is just a metaphor. It can be geographic or demographic. And it can be more than a mile. It can be the world.

THE DRILL

- Define your company's "mile"—the area where you choose to excel. What do you do to "own" or stand out in this mile?

40

SATISFACTION IS A RATING, LOYALTY IS AN EMOTION

A lot of people, and companies, talk about the importance of "customer satisfaction." They're aiming too low!

WE NEVER, EVER WANT to settle for satisfied customers. You know why? Because satisfaction is just a rating—and an average rating, at that. Whenever a customer checks off a "Yes" answer to the question, "Were you satisfied with this purchase/experience/whatever?" all that really proves is that we've fulfilled the minimum requirement to avoid a complaint. We've delivered an average experience, a Moment of Mediocrity—nothing more. We've done nothing to create loyalty.

The very best companies recognize that satisfied customers are not loyal customers. Wherever there's satisfaction, we want to find a way to take that up to the next level, which is an above-average experience. That's what creates positive emotion. Loyalty is rooted in positive emotion, and that usually requires some person-to-person engagement, the kind of engagement that makes the customer think, "I've got to come back here the next time I need so-and-so." That kind of response comes from being more than just "satisfied."

Most people think of customer loyalty as a lifetime, but the reality is that loyalty is all about the next time—every time!

Here's how Bradley, an associate at Bates Ace Hardware in Atlanta, generated the emotion necessary to create loyalty. A local homeowner called on Father's Day and explained that he'd been mowing his lawn when his lawnmower engine had cut out. He'd changed the oil and checked the filter, but he still couldn't manage to get it started again. After a detailed discussion of the problem, Bradley told the gentleman to bring the lawnmower in so he could fix it. The customer did just that; Bradley took the mower and promised a call the next day with an update. Just five hours later, however, Bradley called and told the homeowner he had disassembled the mower, found the problem, replaced a damaged part, and fixed the mower. Total cost: a very reasonable 85 dollars. Bradley made a point of wishing his new customer a "Happy Father's Day" on his way out of the store!

What I want you to notice is that Bradley did not simply "satisfy" this customer's expectations. He dramatically exceeded those expectations. That's what builds positive emotion, loyalty, and evangelism: an above-average experience! The customer posted a glowing, positive review about Bradley's work and attitude that Father's Day. It concluded with these words: "Ace Hardware knows they have to compete with Home Depot, Lowe's, and any other hardware store. Therefore, they go above and beyond in customer service and satisfaction. They are very friendly, understanding, and fast. If you ever have lawnmower problems, call up Bates and you will be taken care of."

That's not just meeting, but exceeding, expectations. That's the kind of service that doesn't just satisfy a customer; it creates loyalty. And, even better, thanks to social media, this customer became an Ace evangelist when he left his glowing feedback for everyone to see!

YOUR AMAZEMENT TOOLBOX

- There's a big difference between a satisfied customer and a loyal customer. Never settle for "satisfied."

- Satisfaction is just a rating—and an average rating, at that. Loyalty is an emotion that ties you to the customer.

- All satisfaction proves is that we've fulfilled the minimum requirement to avoid a complaint.

- Wherever there's satisfaction, we want to find a way to take that up to the next level, to an *above-average* experience.

- Loyalty is rooted in how we engage our customers and their positive emotional reaction to it.

- Loyalty is not about lifetime, although eventually it can be. It's about the next time, every time.

THE DRILL

- Think of a company to which you are truly loyal—the company you love the most. What specific experiences caused you to become a loyal customer?

- Are you aware of any of your current customers who are that loyal to you and your company?

41

BE EASY TO DO BUSINESS WITH

If it's even a little difficult to do business with you, you'd better change the way you do business.

DO YOU HAVE POLICIES, procedures, or rules that get in the way of a customer-first mindset? If you do, it's time to rethink them.

Do you make it easy for customers to process returns and update their orders? If you don't, you'd better be ready to make way for a competitor who does.

Do your people understand that everything they do affects the customer, regardless of their position and responsibility? If they don't, it's time to educate or train them.

Earlier in the book (Tool #15: Adopt a Customer-First Mindset) I introduced you to Matt Dowdell, the Ace retailer in Montana who made a statement about helping "Joe" take care of his to-do list. He referenced tools and machinery, which included computers and any other equipment or technology that could be used to support the customer or streamline the business. The bottom line is that you have to make life easier for "Joe," otherwise, whatever tool, piece of equipment, or system you have in place means nothing.

So here's a great question to ask about your organization, a question that the people at the best Ace stores ask themselves every single day: "Are you easy for Joe to do business with?"

That may sound like a simple question, and you may be tempted to say "Yes" immediately. However, I urge you to take a close look at just how easy and helpful you are perceived to be by your customers and your employees. Ace does this through customer feedback and countless "mystery shopper" exchanges, and it is constantly evaluating the feedback it gets from those shoppers to help improve the customer experience.

Certain companies create an image that they are extremely easy to do business with. (Amazon.com and Apple are two others that come to mind.) Their salespeople, virtual or actual, are friendly. They bend over backwards to take care of you. They provide a "hassle-free" experience. Most people love doing business with a place like this, for two reasons:

1. They really are easy to do business with. They train their people and create systems that actually support the customer. (How soon after you place an order on Amazon do you get an email message saying "thank you"?)

2. They are customer-centric and recognize that every person in the company, regardless of their responsibility, somehow affects the customer. That's the customer-first approach. (How "at home" do you feel at the Apple Store?)

As you interact with customers or work on systems, ask yourself this question:

Is what I'm doing making it easier for the customer?

If not, rethink what you're doing—or getting ready to do.

Look at your business through your customers' eyes. Have you made it as easy as possible for the customer? Or are some of the procedures in place simply for the convenience of your company? Ask your customers. Listen to their answers. Find out ways to improve. The bottom line is, the easier you are to do business with, the happier your customers will be.

YOUR AMAZEMENT TOOLBOX

- If you have policies, procedures, or rules that get in the way of a customer-first mindset, it is time to rethink them.

- Use customer feedback and/or some type of mystery shopping program to identify opportunities for improvement.

- As you interact with a customer, ask yourself, "Is what I'm doing making it easier for the customer?"

THE DRILL

- What are some examples of things that can get in the way of an "easy" buying experience from your company?

42

GET FIRSTHAND EXPERIENCE

How much do you know about the products or services your company sells?

IF YOU WANT TO AMAZE Every Customer Every Time, you need to be perceived as an authority on what you sell. In other words, you need to have some kind of firsthand experience with or knowledge about the products or services you offer the customer.

I don't just mean that you need to be familiar with how much something costs, or what kind of warranty comes with it, or what the outside of the package looks like. That's a good start, but you could do even better. You could actually have personal experience with what you sell, at least for long enough to demo it in the same way that a customer would!

Does this mean that everybody in your organization has to have really deep experience with every single product or service on the list? No. But it does mean that, as one of the people on your team, you should have a broad level of personal exposure to the most popular products and services you sell, and you should be able to truthfully answer, from personal experience, the most common questions customers have.

Admittedly, it may be impossible to know everything, but you do need to know where or from whom to get the answers. And, once you have those answers, you need to know how to communicate the information back to the customer. Knowledge creates credibility and confidence, which are crucial to your success.

The other day I was having dinner at a restaurant and asked the server, "What's the best thing on the menu?" (That's a question a server should be able to answer.)

She paused for a moment, and said, "Oh, the London Broil!"

I saw that she'd hesitated a little before she answered. Curious, I asked, "You're a big fan of the London Broil?"

She grinned sheepishly, and then admitted, "Actually, I haven't eaten anything on the menu yet. I just started yesterday."

The credibility of that server *and* that restaurant just took a major hit! Now, contrast that experience with the one you would receive at a restaurant where the training includes *trying out the most popular menu items on a regular basis*—like, say, every night—so that every single member of the staff can get a sense of what customers like, and why they like it. That's a whole different level of commitment to amazement!

I had an Ace store owner ask me, "You know why people in my neighborhood buy a Big Green Egg from me?" (By the way, a Big Green Egg is a very fancy—and expensive—barbecue pit.)

I said, "No, why?"

He said, "Because I'm the Big Green Egg Guru! I don't just sell the Big Green Egg; I don't just show you how to put it together; and I don't just tie it down in the back of your pickup truck once it's assembled. I also make sure you get the very best recipes, and before you drive off, I give you a taste of some of the steak I just cooked with it!" He wasn't kidding. He knows his stuff!

If you go to an Ace store, I bet you are going to run into someone who knows his or her stuff. Most of the associates will have a certain area of specialty, and some of them will have deep professional experience in a given area. Maybe the guy in the electrical department used to be an electrician. The place is full of people with personal experience and expertise in particular areas of interest to customers.

The very best companies will either hire the right people who *already* know how to use a certain product or service that they sell, or they will give them the training they need to have that knowledge and experience. They make sure the right people are able to be *helpful* to customers who have questions. If your company isn't doing that, it should!

Remember: Not everybody needs to be trained in everything. You can be an expert in one area and not another. If you don't know the answers to your customers' questions, you should know who to go to or call to get those answers. Customers love to do business with people who know what they're talking about. It gives them confidence, and customer confidence can lead to loyalty.

You may not be the person with all the answers about the Big Green Egg, but you should know who is, and you should be able to tell a customer how and when to connect with that person.

YOUR AMAZEMENT TOOLBOX

- Making good recommendations to customers, based on personal experience, gives you and your company credibility.

- People with relevant product/service experience should get the opportunity to help customers who have questions.

- You may not know all of the answers about a given product, but you should know where or who to go to to get the answers.

THE DRILL

- When was the last time you helped a customer by using your own personal knowledge of, and experience with, the product or service you sell?

- How often do you get to take your company's products or services "out for a test drive"?

43

SHOW YOUR GRATITUDE

Show your best customers how grateful you are for their continued business by delivering a superb "THANK YOU" experience!

A CONSULTANT FRIEND OF MINE makes a point of sending his "top-tier" clients a special gift of baked goods just to thank them for choosing to do repeat business with him. The pastries, which are homemade from a special family recipe, serve as a thoughtful reminder of the consultant's long-term gratitude for the client's choice to work with him on an ongoing basis. The positive buying experience he delivers is one thing; the positive service experience he delivers is another thing. And this special "gratitude after-experience" takes it to a whole new level, by letting his key clients know that he really, truly appreciates their business. Because he does!

There are many ways to say thank you to a customer: a verbal acknowledgment at the end of the interaction, an email, a follow-up phone call, and even a handwritten note—or by going above and beyond, as demonstrated in this next example.

In Seattle there's an Ace Hardware store with a particularly happy customer named Bonnie who's like family to the store associates. She has been buying from the store for quite a long time. One day, Bonnie asked for some help in selecting the perfect paint color for her bathroom. The Ace associate she asked for help happened to have a college background in art and knew a lot about color selection. So, she spent a significant amount of time with Bonnie, walking her through all the possible color selections and helping her to plot out the very best design choices for her room.

The two of them spent a lot of time on this seemingly simple painting project. Before long, it actually started to look more like a major consulting assignment! Bonnie thanked her salesperson, but it was the salesperson who was emphatic about expressing appreciation for the opportunity to serve. Of course, that's what Ace people do. They provide the most *helpful* service on the planet, taking the time necessary to make sure that their customers get what they want and need.

Pretty impressive, right? You might think that that's the end of a very nice customer service story. But there is more. Once the customer made it home and started painting, she realized that the project just wasn't unfolding in the way that she and the Ace associate had envisioned it. There was something wrong with the color, but she couldn't figure out what it was. She reached out to the Ace associate, who actually dropped by her home for a house call!

By looking closely at the house's color scheme, *in person*, the Ace associate was able to tweak the bathroom color selections until they really were perfect—and also send a favored customer an unforgettable message of customer service that truly went "above and beyond." That's Ace's way of showing gratitude. By Amazing Customers Every Time!

YOUR AMAZEMENT TOOLBOX

- Show your best customers how grateful you are for their continued business. Send a token of your gratitude.

- Follow up to deliver a superb "gratitude" experience that exceeds your customers' (high) expectations!

- Sometimes showing gratitude is delivering the most amazing customer service experience ever!

- You don't have to write a thank-you note to show gratitude. You can do it by providing an *above and beyond* customer experience.

THE DRILL

- When have you showed a customer, through both words and actions, just how grateful you were for his or her business?

- Who was the customer?

- How did you show that gratitude?

44

DON'T LEAVE LOYALTY TO CHANCE

De-commoditize your business so you can start winning and keeping customers!

A RECENT POLL PUBLISHED in *TIME* magazine (November 12, 2012) was a real eye-opener. The poll, commissioned by Parature, a customer service software company, said that poor customer service costs US companies about $80 billion a year in lost sales, and that 60 percent of those unhappy customers end up going to a competitor.

Now, there are two ways to respond to these numbers. One way is to say, "My goodness—we'd better not be among those companies that are hemorrhaging customers. We'd better make darned sure that our customers are so consistently amazed they don't even *think* about defecting to the competition."

That is definitely a good response. There's also a second good response we should consider making. It sounds like this: "My goodness—there's $80-billion worth of unsatisfied customers out there. More than half of them are going to end up choosing someone new to work with. How do we make sure that we get our share of those customers?"

The very best way to get your share of the (huge) portion of potential buyers out there who are willing to switch over to you is *not to leave their service experience to chance.* That means consciously delivering an above-average experience, from the customer's point of view, every single time.

It doesn't matter whether you are a business-to-consumer or business-to-business type of company. You can do this. Depending on the type of business and industry you are in, the numbers may vary, but the concept is valid. The reality remains that many customers will spend more for a better experience. Delivering an amazing experience takes you out of the commodity-driven, price-sensitive corner of whatever industry you happen to be in. Don't leave the customer experience to chance! Design an experience that the customers who have been alienated by your competition will appreciate, remember, and come back to experience again.

Maybe you're wondering: What does "not leaving the experience to chance" look like in action? Well, consider Ace, which steadfastly refuses to leave the customer experience to chance. That's because they know, based on plenty of in-person customer feedback and plenty of surveys, exactly what situations are likely to frustrate a hardware store customer enough to consider giving up on the big-box competition and coming over to Ace. One of those situations is: *Having one—just one!—project on your to-do list to take care of, and not getting the help you need to complete it so you can get back to other things you want or need to do.*

Because the people at Ace know that they have to deliver an experience that is the exact opposite of that frustration, the most successful stores consistently implement a very simple best practice. No matter what else happens during your visit, an Ace associate will *notice you, interact with you, make sure you find what you're looking for, and ask you how you're planning to use it—the goal being that you get everything you need on your first visit so you don't have to come back to the store.*

That's a core best practice at Ace. You'll find that Ace people have been trained to execute it in virtually every interaction with a customer! That might sound simple and intuitive, but it's something that typically does not happen to you when you visit one of Ace's competitors. This level of *helpful* is what separates Ace from its competition.

Caley, an Ace customer in Colorado, described the motives behind this kind of high-value purchase experience as follows: "Usually, when I hit the hardware store, I am already frustrated from my project. It's nice to have a store where they make it easy to get what you need, pleasantly, and get on your way." That's loyalty talking right there. That's a customer experience that has not been left to chance!

You want to deliver a *de-commoditizing* experience, the kind of experience that gets customers to switch, and be happy they did.

YOUR AMAZEMENT TOOLBOX

- Poor customer service costs US companies about $80 billion a year in lost sales. (Parature study, 2012)

- 60 percent of customers unhappy with a company's customer service will end up switching to a competitor.

- Delivering an amazing experience takes you out of the commodity-driven, price-sensitive corner of your industry.

- Don't leave the customer experience to chance. Be deliberate about the value you provide to customers.

- Know what frustrates customers enough to make them want to switch to a competitor. Then, deliver the opposite experience.

THE DRILL

- Is your customer experience so much better than your competitors' that your best customers are willing to pay a little more?

- If so, what exactly are you doing to make the price less relevant? If not, what can you do?

45

DO WHAT IS NOT EXPECTED

Be on the lookout for opportunities to do what you know the competition would not do.

EARLIER WE DEFINED AN AMAZING level of customer service as service that is consistently above average. I always emphasize to the clients I work with and the audiences I talk to that, in order to be amazing, you don't have to deliver WOW service every single time. You just have to be consistently above average.

However . . .

Truly great companies are still always *on the lookout* for opportunities to deliver that WOW experience—by doing something they know the competition would not do. They don't necessarily expect to deliver that level of service every time, but when they see the chance, they try to take advantage of it. That builds intense loyalty and enthusiastic evangelists for the brand. (See the epilogue: "Create a Demanding Customer.")

Jerry Campbell, manager of an Ace store in Dayton, Ohio, had a customer come in and ask for a particular type of shower head, one that had to be special ordered and mailed to her home. Curious, Campbell asked the customer why she didn't want to just come by to pick the order up. As it turned out, she didn't have a car, and her apartment was located a long way from the nearest bus stop. The cab ride to and from the Ace store was ten dollars each way, and that was a lot of money.

"That's no problem," Jerry said. "When the order comes in, we'll give you a call, and then I or one of the associates here can swing by your apartment after work and drop off the shower head."

The customer's response was an enthusiastic, "Well, that would be awfully nice!"

Wow! Would the competition do that? It's doubtful. Jerry had spotted and acted on an opportunity to do something the customer *did not expect*.

When the shower head came in, Jerry called the customer, set up a time to come by, dropped off her order, and picked up the money. Here's the point: This customer was amazed at the service she received. More than just a regular customer, she became an active evangelist for Ace, telling all of her neighbors about her experience, which turned into more business. And why did this happen? Because Jerry did something his competitors most likely would not do. By now you know—that's how Ace competes. They know what others don't and won't do, and they take advantage of that knowledge. That's how you stand out. That's how you become amazing!

YOUR AMAZEMENT TOOLBOX

- Delivering customer amazement doesn't mean you have to deliver wow service every time. Just be consistently better than average.

- When you see the chance to do something the competition definitely would not do, consider taking advantage of it.

- Look for opportunities to create Moments of Magic that the customer *does not expect*.

THE DRILL

- Have you ever taken advantage of an opportunity to surprise the customer with something that he or she didn't expect? What was it?

- How did the customer react?

46

DELIVER AMAZING FOLLOW-UP

Following up with the customer after the sale establishes confidence that can lead to loyalty.

WHENEVER YOU CREATE a customer service experience that results in a decision to purchase your product or service, you automatically have a new opportunity for amazement. It's what I call amazing follow-up, an *after-experience* that is a powerful tool to reinforce that the customer made the right choice to buy from you.

For example, a friend of mine bought a new home, and several days after he moved in, he got a call from his real estate agent. The agent just wanted to make sure everything was going well and also wanted to find out whether there was anything my friend needed. (The call itself is positive follow-up No. 1!) During the call, the agent mentioned that he had a special gift for every family with small children who buys a home from him. The agency owns a bounce house, one of those huge blow-up houses that kids (and some parents) climb into and bounce around in. My friend's ears perked up; his daughter had her eighth birthday coming up. As one of the real estate agent's clients, my friend was free to use it for a day. (That gift is positive follow-up No. 2!)

A follow-up like that becomes part of the experience days, weeks, or even months after the actual purchase. This positive follow-up reinforces the customer's original decision to do business with you—and exceeds the customer's expectations. That's what makes it amazing!

You can do this in any number of ways. It can be the follow-up phone call or a thank-you note. (See Tool #43: Show Your Gratitude.) Maybe you send a customer a special article on something related to the specific product or service that he or she just bought. Perhaps it's an email with a link to a video that the manufacturer produced especially for new users.

Some of the Ace stores are known for regularly executing this strategy as a way to create value and build an even stronger relationship with their customers. I've heard and read so many stories of personal follow-up after a decision to purchase from an Ace store that I couldn't possibly have included them all in this book. I do want to draw special attention to one story, though. Stephen placed an order for an electric fence kit at Ace-Hardware.com, which is Ace's online shopping portal. After he bought his fence, he received not one, not two, but three separate calls from his local Ace store to confirm the order and confirm that it actually showed up when he needed it. Admittedly, this may seem extreme, but in this case it was totally appropriate. Not many online (or even brick-and-mortar) vendors offer that kind of amazing follow-up!

YOUR AMAZEMENT TOOLBOX

- Unexpected follow-up after the sale is a great way to amaze your customer.

- Connect your follow-up contact with the original purchase to make it truly amazing.

- Following up with your customer reinforces that the customer made the right decision to do business with you.

THE DRILL

- Think of a time you followed up with a customer after the sale. What did you do?

- How could you use this follow-up approach with other customers?

47

STAY IN TOUCH

Promote yourself and your company by staying in touch on a consistent basis.

IN THE LAST TOOL, we covered how to deliver amazing follow-up. This tool, however, describes a different type of follow-up in that it's not specifically tied to a sale. It's not a thank-you note or a follow-up phone call. It's about staying in touch in between sales.

This tool is about staying in touch with your customers by creating a series of regular touch points. These touch points should show that you are interested in maintaining and growing your professional relationship. Such consistent interactions with your customers create what marketing and advertising people call creating "top-of-mind awareness."

This simple idea probably has one of the highest returns on investment in terms of generating and sustaining engagement and loyalty, yet it only takes a little bit of effort and time. The key is to use this approach with your existing customers—the ones who already know and love you. Find a way to stay connected, even if they don't do business with you very often.

There are many ways to do this. You can send the customer a newsletter by mail or email, write a personalized note, or send something of personal interest, such as an article from a magazine that you know would interest certain customers.

Perhaps the most powerful touch point of all is simply to call up to say hello every month or so and let the customer know you've been thinking of him or her. While this may technically be a sales call, the main point is to make it personal. You are checking in with your customers, finding out how they are doing, and *then* mentioning that there are some specials or new products they may be interested in knowing about. For example, about twice a year my wife receives a call from a salesperson at a store where she likes to shop. The sales rep knows what my wife likes and lets her know about the new clothes that are coming in that she might be interested in.

I have a friend who is a car dealer who takes a more subtle approach. He sends a monthly email to his customers and friends that includes timely tips, such as a reminder to turn your clocks forward for daylight saving time, or to remember to check the batteries in your smoke detectors. Not once has he ever tried to sell a car in any of these emails. That's important to notice! This may be one of the most powerful ways of utilizing this tool. While it seems like he isn't promoting anything, he is actually promoting himself. His goal is simple: whenever you become interested in a car, he wants to be top of mind.

At least once a month, I email a newsletter to my clients. This always includes an article I've written on customer service. I've never sent out the newsletter with blatant promotion or advertising. I make a point of building the newsletter around value-added content that my clients appreciate.

Ace executes this touch point principle very well by sending out a monthly e-newsletter to customers who sign up on the AceHardware.com website or are members of the Ace Rewards program. The Ace Hardware e-newsletter is packed with great home improvement and maintenance advice, customized to the preferences of the subscriber. A lot of local stores create their own e-newsletters, targeted specifically to the local community. In addition to the typical maintenance, repair, and home improvement advice, local retailers send information about storms approaching their area and what to do to prepare. They can also alert customers when a bug, weed, or fungus hits the area.

Gene Pedrotti of Pedrotti's Ace Hardware in Benicia, California, is a master at keeping in touch with his customers. He sends them emails linking to how-to videos he posts on YouTube for his customers to view. Three years ago he had an opportunity to buy several hundred holiday wreaths at a very low price because they were overstocked at the warehouse. He sent them to his top 400 customers as a holiday gift. Every year Gene takes the time to mail a personal, handwritten note to these same top customers. What a powerful way to stay in touch!

Please don't think this is just about the company. This is also an excellent personal strategy that, while promoting the company you work for, will also promote you as an individual and endears you to the customer. It's a pattern of connections that delivers more than the customer expects. Keep it up, and your customers will start to consider you amazing!

YOUR AMAZEMENT TOOLBOX

- Consistently staying in touch with customers creates what advertising and marketing people call "top-of-mind awareness."

- Consider setting up a monthly e-newsletter that is focused on value for the customer versus blatant promotion.

- One of the most powerful touch points is to call customers just to let them know you are thinking of them.

- The most effective regular touch points are the ones that do not try to sell anything.

THE DRILL

- Are there certain customers that you, or your company, stay in touch with on a regular basis? How do you go about doing it (phone calls, emails, newsletters, etc.)?

48

GET PROACTIVE

Being proactive for the customer means solving problems before they start!

HAVE YOU EVER BEEN in a restaurant where the waiter refilled your glass of water before you even had to ask? If you have, then you've experienced proactive service. There's never an empty water glass, so you never have to catch the waiter's attention to come fill it.

A lot of people aren't used to thinking of problem solving in this way. Typically, we wait until a customer has a complaint or a problem, then we take ownership of it and work out a solution that leaves the customer remembering a Moment of Magic, rather than a Moment of Misery.

Don't get me wrong; that's certainly a good outcome (see Tool #35: Master the Art of Recovery). But there is an even better approach: *proactive* service, the kind of service that keeps problems from materializing in the first place!

Getting into problem-solving mode is good, and it's certainly necessary sometimes. But getting into *proactive* mode, so that there isn't even a problem to deal with in the first place, is even better. For example, it may be that the shipping department follows up with a customer to make sure the package arrived instead of waiting to hear from the customer that it didn't.

Doesn't that make perfect sense? After all, customers decide to do business with you because they trust you. Proactive service reinforces their decision to do business with you. It helps to build respect, confidence, loyalty, and evangelism for your brand. Why leave this powerful concept to chance? Make it a normal procedure, as part of the greeting, sales, and follow-up process!

The idea of proactive service is not new. It's been around for decades. Often, though, what I find is that there is *no formal process in place* at most companies to provide the type of "thinking ahead" that prevents customers from having to identify and take action on their own problems.

Usually, we don't have a set of steps in place that keeps people from reaching the point where they say, "Hey, my water glass is empty—where's that waiter?" (As it were.) To continue with the example of the restaurant, there are attentive waiters and inattentive waiters, but there usually isn't a standard that makes sure that *every* waiter in the restaurant notices half-empty water glasses every time. It is usually an individual employee's effort and initiative that provides this high level of service. It's quite rare that a company invests in, trains for, and supports a truly proactive customer experience.

Ace Hardware stores are a world-class model for this approach. Different Ace stores do this in different ways, of course—that's the beauty of the Ace model, which is built on the principle of autonomy for the individual stores. Nevertheless, they each have certain best practices they can follow to deliver proactive service. It can be as simple as a greeting at the front of the store and a question about what the customer is looking for. Shannon Carney's store in California has taken this *helpful* best practice of greeting the customer to a much higher level, though. Her front-of-store greeter has the title of Customer Coordinator (CC) and acts as "floor director." The CC greets the customers, asks them what they're looking for, and directs them to the proper aisle in the store. All of the associates are equipped with wireless radio headsets, and it's the CC's job to inform team members about what parts of the store the customers are headed toward, when a customer needs help, when a customer doesn't want help, when a customer is in a hurry, and much more. Imagine going to the electrical section and there is an Ace associate waiting for you when you get there. That's proactive service in action—because the "empty glass" (a customer wandering around the store looking for help) is never allowed to happen in the first place!

YOUR AMAZEMENT TOOLBOX

- Proactive service is the ability to head off problems before they happen.

- Proactive service is an opportunity to show how good you really are.

- Proactive service reinforces the decision the customer made. It helps to build respect, confidence, and loyalty.

- Make proactive service a normal procedure as part of the greeting, sales, and follow-up process, and watch your customers say, "Wow!"

THE DRILL

- Were you ever able to *prevent* a problem from happening, or anticipate a customer's needs before he or she asked for something? How did you do that?

CHAPTER TEN

COMMUNITY

"We make a living by what we get, but we make a life by what we give."

—WINSTON CHURCHILL

CHURCHILL COULDN'T HAVE REALIZED IT, but he was expressing, with perfect faithfulness, the philosophy that truly sets Ace Hardware apart in each of the communities where it operates.

We close this part of the book with an essential reminder, one that distinguishes the most amazing companies from everyone else. Business and success are not just about us.

True success happens when we start to look beyond the short-term outcomes that immediately benefit ourselves and our business. The strongest loyalty of all is the loyalty that's rooted in being a member of the same community that the customer belongs to. The final four Amazement Tools (#s 49–52) show you how to build much stronger ties to that community.

Community Tools

49. The Law of Reciprocity

50. Do Local Well

51. Loyalty Goes Both Ways

52. Be Part of Something Bigger than Yourself

49

THE LAW OF RECIPROCITY

The more you give, the more you get.

PERHAPS YOU'VE HEARD that saying before. It's known as the Law of Reciprocity. You help people get what they want, and in return, somehow it comes back to you. It may not happen at that moment or with that person, but it comes back. And, this is an overarching strategy—or maybe a better word, "philosophy"—of Ace Hardware.

I've interviewed dozens and dozens of Ace Hardware owners, executives, and associates, and one of the topics that comes up over and over again is their commitment to their community.

This local commitment to improve the community, to make things better, takes countless different forms, financial and otherwise, and it serves countless diverse groups of people. Because Ace stores are independently owned and operated, there is no requirement to "give back" to the community. Headquarters doesn't tell everyone in the Ace network that it's time to write out a check to the local branch of such-and-such charity. Instead, charity *the Ace way* is all about what makes sense to the owner of the individual store, the people who work in the store and live in the area. It might be the sponsorship of a Little League team, or support for the local shelter for the homeless, or a decision to pull out the chainsaws, fire up the pickup trucks, and help clear local streets and driveways after a storm. Or it might be a combination of all of these.

The point is, you won't see a uniform approach when it comes to fulfilling this value of giving something back to the community that an individual Ace store serves. In fact, at a very few stores, you might not see charitable giving emphasized in any obvious way. Here again, though, we're interested in what *usually* happens *most* of the time across the store network. And what usually happens is that the people within the store find a way to make a big positive impact on the lives of people who may be in need.

Ace's former Chairman of the Board, Tom Glenn, told me that it sometimes comes as a surprise to outsiders, and even to newcomers to the Ace family, to learn that this kind of giving is one of the big reasons that store owners in the Ace network strive to do well financially—and succeed! They want to be successful enough to start making some decisions that *don't* support their bottom line.

"What you find when you talk to our people who are the most successful," he told me, "is that a lot of them want to be able to have a store that performs well enough in terms of their own margin for them to be in a position to make some major investments in the community where they live. Those investments reduce the margin, but that's okay. That's why they wanted to build the margin up in the first place. That's a big motivator for them, a big reason why they get up in the morning and do what they do every day, the potential to make their own community a better place."

Mind you, I'm not saying that Ace is a charitable organization. These are businesses, and they operate in order to get and keep customers. What I am saying, though, is that a whole lot of Ace stores have built their brand promise into something that's a little bigger than a hardware store, something that has the potential to inspire everyone who comes in contact with it on the local level: a true commitment to the community. That community starts with the family of the owner, extends out through the associates who work at the store, and eventually includes everyone in the store's immediate area—whether or not they ever buy anything from Ace!

You might be tempted to think that your local Ace store does what it does for your community "just to get good coverage in the local news" or "just to get their store's name out there." You might be tempted to think this is all a little opportunistic around the edges. And, you're right. There is no doubt that publicity and goodwill are a benefit to giving back. That's why this tool is called The Law of Reciprocity.

Rick Alspaugh, an Ace owner in Kingwood, Texas, uses most of his marketing budget for local charities and his community. There isn't a Little League team, a bake sale, or a school or charitable event that he doesn't contribute to. Everyone knows him. His store is deeply interwoven with the community in lots of different ways. By giving, the community reciprocates with loyalty. That's a competitive edge. Rick feels this is a great way to give back—and get back. This is the Law of Reciprocity in action!

But, after having talked to many members of the Ace family over the years, I'd be more inclined to say that your local store does what it does for your community because it's all about delivering on *helpful.* It's the belief that, when someone at Ace makes the decision to take good care of you, as one member of the community to another, *good things start happening to everybody.*

Zig Ziglar, the incomparable motivational speaker, once said, "You will get all you want in life if you help other people get what *they* want." A lot of people have repeated that advice over the years. Zig was right, of course! He was reminding us all of the power of the Law of Reciprocity.

YOUR AMAZEMENT TOOLBOX

- Be so successful that you don't have to make every decision based on what's best for the bottom line.

- Look for ways to make a positive impact on the lives of people in need.

- When you take care of the community, good things happen to everybody!

- Zig Ziglar said, "You will get all you want out of life if you help other people get what *they* want." That's the Law of Reciprocity.

THE DRILL

- What does your company do to give back to the community?

- When was the last time you personally had a positive impact on the life of someone who was in need? (Use examples from inside or outside the workplace.)

50

DO LOCAL WELL

No matter how big you get, don't get too big to care about the local community.

EARLIER IN THE BOOK (Tool #16: Celebrate Uniqueness) I introduced you to the notion of respecting and embracing the uniqueness of the people you work with. The way you can tell that you've successfully implemented this tool is that your team members start doing a better job of embracing and celebrating the uniqueness of individual customers—and, by extension, the local community.

When we accept each other as we are, we do a better job of accepting customers as they are. We take a little more time to connect with those who buy from us—and even those who don't! If we all *celebrate uniqueness* well, we will be operating as far as anyone can get from the cookie-cutter business model that can leave customers with a cold, impersonal feeling. We become a major strategic asset for the business, the means by which the company *does local well.*

Ace is a global company with more than 4,600 stores in 70 different countries, and its entire helpful business model depends on doing local well. It is a successful international brand made up of thousands of locally owned businesses operating as local players in local marketplaces. Each one of those businesses is driven by deep local ties within that marketplace as it operationalizes helpful in its own unique way. If I were building a

208

global brand, that's the kind of brand I would want to build. *Global in philosophy and culture, local in execution and relationships.*

There's a big difference between a national or an international company with a true local presence, as compared to a national company with a local branch that's "just following orders" from headquarters. If you want to be like Ace, that means you want to be a national or an international brand that also operates a truly local and customer-focused business. You want to have connections to the community that run very deep—so deep that you can never say, "It's not my department, call corporate."

And you know what? If you're an Ace customer, you won't ever get that kind of response from a local Ace owner, manager, or associate. Why? Because they are members of the community they serve. They know that the buck stops with them, and they communicate that message to the community by the way they treat their customers.

In New York City, there's an Ace store that hired a graffiti artist to do the in-store decorations. That kind of move wouldn't make a lot of sense to hardware store customers in Minot, North Dakota, but in the Big Apple, the graffiti designs send a perfect message: "You've come to the right place. We understand you because . . . we are you."

YOUR AMAZEMENT TOOLBOX

- Be global in philosophy and culture but local in execution and relationships. "Do local well."

- Never say, "It's not my department, call corporate." Instead say, "You're here, in our store. You've come to the right place."

- The way your community thinks about you depends on the way you treat your customers.

THE DRILL

- Think of a local store or restaurant where you really enjoy shopping or eating. How does this business make you feel like you are a *local* or a *regular*?

- What can you do to give your company a more "local" feel (especially if your company is large, national, or international)?

51

LOYALTY GOES BOTH WAYS

Don't expect customers to be loyal to you before you are loyal to them.

SOME COMPANIES' "CUSTOMER LOYALTY" PROGRAMS are more like "customer entrapment" programs. They don't reward you for your loyalty. They punish you if you aren't loyal. For example, they may have rules in which you forfeit all of your points or credits if you don't give them enough business. Some of my friends tell me the only reason they fly a particular airline is because they have so many miles accrued in their loyalty program, and they don't want to lose them. Otherwise, they would switch. Is that loyalty?

The point is that they don't have loyalty to the company. They have loyalty to the loyalty program. That's a big difference.

In order to get our customers to be loyal to us, we need to be loyal to our customers first.

Loyalty is about creating value at the personal level for your customer. It's about building a strong relationship and developing trust. It's about having an understanding of our customers' world, knowing what they want and need, making them feel special, and letting them know we appreciate them—and that we are there for them. Once they know we're there for them, they'll be there for us. *Loyalty goes both ways, and it starts with us.*

Steve Kelly, Director of Store Operations for the Ace stores in Chattanooga, Tennessee, is someone who knows that loyalty goes both ways. When his community was hit by a massive snowstorm that left over a foot and a half of snow on the ground, he made sure all of his stores stayed open, even though all the other businesses in town were shut down. Steve knew most of his customers personally, and he knew that they were going to need things like shovels and flashlights and batteries and generators.

So, the store managers and the associates spent the night in the stores just to be absolutely sure that they were open when people in the community needed them. (Steve spent the night in one of them too.) This decision of Steve's wasn't about making a lot of money, and it certainly wasn't about raising prices to take advantage of a neighbor's inconvenience. It was (as he put it) about "being there for our community in a time of need."

That's the very best loyalty program there is. And you don't have to wait for a snowstorm to start it. You can launch a real loyalty program just by taking full advantage of the next opportunity to deliver *helpful* to your customer.

YOUR AMAZEMENT TOOLBOX

- A true loyalty program rewards loyal customers versus enticing customers to do business with us, which is marketing.

- Don't confuse customers who are loyal to your company with customers who are just loyal to your loyalty program.

- In order to get our customers to be loyal to us, we need to be loyal to our customers first.

- Be there for your customers and your community, especially in a time of need.

- The best way to start a loyalty program is to be there for your customers and your community, always.

THE DRILL

- How do you or your company show loyalty to your customers?

- Identify a time when you and/or your company made a point of "being there" for customers and the larger community, especially in a time of need. What role did you play in that experience?

52

BE PART OF SOMETHING BIGGER THAN YOURSELF

Helpful is more than a business strategy. It is a philosophy that touches the human spirit.

WE CLOSE WITH THE CHALLENGE that the greatest careers and the greatest companies manage to meet: True success, for both people and companies, comes when we commit ourselves to helping others. This is more than helping our customers with our products. It's much bigger than that. I touched on this idea in Tool #49: The Law of Reciprocity, and I want to end the book by exploring it more deeply here, because I believe it is the highest-ranking "card" any person or organization committed to great service can play.

Over and over again, while doing research for this book, I asked executives, owners, associates, and customers of the most helpful hardware stores on the planet to tell me what made Ace different from other businesses. The same two answers always came up: *people* and *community*. Ace Hardware achieves the goals of "putting people first" and "giving to the community" by weaving them deep into the DNA of its business.

Tom Knox, Ace's Vice President of Retail and Business Development, put it this way:

Ace's success is rooted in something that's a whole lot bigger than anything you can buy at a store. We're really more than just a store, and what we're doing every day is something a lot more important than just selling hardware. We are part of the community, and we really do build our day around giving something back to that community because we live there too. That's the secret. We're part of something that's bigger than any one of us.

Now, a lot of people on the outside of the business think we're focused on helpful, and from their perspective, we are. But when you spend some time with us, you realize that what we are really focused on is family—the Ace family. It happens to be a pretty big family, a global family, and we are so proud to be part of it that we're always looking for new ways to take care of each other. That's why you see people in the community relying on us the way they do. It's the way we take care of each other. I believe that, as long we can still inspire our people to look beyond themselves and take care of the family, we'll continue to be successful.

Gene Pedrotti, owner of Pedrotti Ace Hardware in Benicia, California, told me: "People sometimes ask me why I am so devoted to Ace Hardware. The answer is that I believe we're here not just to serve ourselves and our associates, but to serve our community at a higher level . . . You don't look for ways to treat people like friends. You look for ways to treat people like family. I believe you can expand that family to include the whole world if you want to."

Dozens of members of the Ace retail family I talked to shared moving stories of how their people stepped up to help their communities during natural catastrophes such as hurricanes, floods, and tornadoes. They took chainsaws and cut up tree limbs that were blocking roads. They kept their stores open 24 hours a day for people who needed them to be there. They took their own personal time to band together with their teammates for the betterment of the community.

This fusion of business and community gives customers, associates, owners, and everyone else who comes in contact with the organization an inspiring sense of achieving something more important than any individual could possibly achieve independently. Charitable giving is a part of that achievement. For example, Ace is very involved in the Children's Miracle Network and numerous other charities, but that's only part of it. Philanthropy isn't all we're talking about here. The word "neighborhood" does a better job of describing what Ace actually supports with its mission. Make sure your business is part of a neighborhood (whether it's virtual or geographical), a special community where people look out for each other.

At the best Ace stores, you experience a sense of being part of something shared, something that matters, something about mutual trust and looking out for each other that used to be much more common in our world, something that is worth keeping around. Maureen, a long-time Ace customer in Washington State, posted these memorable words online in praise of her local Ace store: *"You define what it means to live in a community."*

Our own willingness to give something back to our community is the best measure of our success in this world. That's the real Ace card, the highest-ranking card in the deck, and it's the card we should be ready and willing to play.

YOUR AMAZEMENT TOOLBOX

- We can always find a way to be part of something bigger than ourselves, and we will always be glad we did.

- Integrate "putting people first" and "giving to the community" by weaving them deep into the DNA of your business.

- Treat your customers like neighbors. Neighbors look out for one another.

- Inspire employees, customers, and everyone else who comes in contact with you to become part of a cause that matters.

- Our own willingness to find a way to HELP each and every person we encounter is the ultimate and best measure of our success.

THE DRILL

- How do you define community?

- What do you and/or your organization give back to the community? Or what could you give back?

CREATE A DEMANDING CUSTOMER

The ultimate test of customer amazement: Be SO GOOD that you create a problem for the competition.

UP TO THIS POINT, I've shared 52 Amazement Tools for Amazing Every Customer Every Time. Some of those tools probably seemed more relevant to your world than others.

Here's what I want you to do now: Pick out the strategies that leapt right out at you, right away, and made you think, "Hey, I—or we—could do that." Make a commitment to start implementing them right now . . . so that within the NEXT 30 DAYS you will have put those initial Amazement Tools into practice and raised the standards of your customers so high that you create a problem for your competition.

One month from now, I want you to be so good at what you do that if one of your customers happened to call on your most significant competitor and requested the same level of service that you deliver, that competitor would consider your customer to be "too demanding."

Notice that I'm talking about a different kind of *demanding customer*. Not one who whines, nags, or is "high maintenance," but one, who loves your service and demands it of others. When you're so good that you meet and exceed the high expectations you set with your customers, you make it harder for your competition to compete with you. These customers aren't demanding of *you*. They are demanding of your competitors, so much so that your competitors aren't up to the task of consistently meeting their demands. That's a great place to be!

Guess what? Demanding customers are less price-sensitive than other customers are. Even in a so-called challenging economy, there are plenty of customers out there who are willing to give you a little wiggle room on price, or maybe even more than a little wiggle room . . .

> IF you do what Ace does, and consistently deliver an above-average experience. That's *amazement!*

> IF you do what Ace does and engage, one-on-one, with your customers and create an emotional bond with each of them.

> IF you do what Ace does, and use the (inevitable) Moments of Misery that arise as opportunities to prove to your customer that you are willing to take responsibility for the problem and find a solution that works for everyone. That turns a Moment of Misery into a Moment of Magic!

> IF you do what Ace does, and go above and beyond the call on behalf of the relationship with the customer, never taking the easy way out.

> IF you do all that, then one month from today your customers will have gotten used to the higher standard you've set. And they'll start to expect it from everyone!

In the end, that's what really de-commoditizes your business: the heightened expectation that creates a demanding customer. Nothing else!

Of course, this is a major part of Ace's business strategy. They want demanding customers, especially the type we're describing here. In fact, the more demanding, the better. As an Ace customer in Seattle put it, "Even though the prices can be, but are not necessarily, higher . . . the convenience and help are worth it." That's a customer who's been *amazed!* You'll hear variations on that message of loyalty, high expectation, and evangelism expressed by countless loyal Ace customers around the world. Ace wins because they strive to be the most *helpful* hardware stores on the planet . . . by creating demanding customers!

YOUR AMAZEMENT TOOLBOX

- Be so good at what you do that when your customers expect the same level of service from a competitor, they're considered too demanding!

- Demanding customers are less price-sensitive than other customers are.

- Even in a "challenging" economy, there are plenty of customers who are willing to accept a higher (but still fair) price, if you *amaze* them.

- Win in the marketplace . . . by creating a demanding customer!

THE DRILL

- Are you so good at what you do that if one of your customers happened to do business with a competitor and demanded the same level of service, that competitor would consider your customer to be "too demanding"?

- If yes, please describe why. If not, what would it take to be that good?

FINAL WORDS

THIS ISN'T THE END of the journey. It's only the beginning.

If all you do is read the ideas I've shared with you about amazement, the journey hasn't pointed you in the right direction. On the other hand, if you make the effort to implement one or more of these 52 tools, you will find that that effort has the potential to transform you and your entire organization.

I've prepared a special companion workbook to go along with this book. It puts all of the questions at the end of each tool into a workbook format that is designed to help you make absolutely sure that you identify the Amazement Tools that are right for you and your organization, and then use those tools in a way that is perfectly suited to your organization and your situation. To download it (free) all you have to do is visit:

www.AmazeEveryCustomer.com

Along with the workbook, you will also find additional content that will help you continue your journey toward amazement.

Always be amazing!
Shep Hyken

ACKNOWLEDGMENTS

FIRST, I WANT TO ACKNOWLEDGE you, the reader. Thank you for investing in this book, which is filled with ideas that can be put to use immediately. My hope is that you picked up many of these ideas from the 52 tools, and if you haven't already done so, will implement them soon. As I stated in the first chapter, it only takes one idea to transform your business.

I owe much gratitude to the clients I get to work with every day. Thank you for the confidence you display when you book me to speak at your meetings, let us provide you with our trusted trainers to help create a customer-focused culture, and, of course, buy my books! Every time I work with a client I learn something new. There is a piece of all of you in this book.

A special thank-you to the team that helped bring this book to the marketplace. Brandon Toropov was my content editor and sounding board, keeping me focused to create a great product. Linda Read helped with initial proofreading and grammatical editing. My team at Greenleaf Book Group was wonderful. There's the CEO, Clint Greenleaf; my main contact, Justin Branch; my day-to-day contact, Alan Grimes; editor extraordinaire, Lari Bishop; cover and interior designer, Kim Lance; and the rest of the team who does everything necessary to create a successful book.

And a huge thank-you to my friends at Ace Hardware. I've been fortunate to be booked as a speaker at their conventions since the 1990s. I'm honored and flattered that they had the confidence in me to produce a book that singles them out as the consummate role model for creating amazing customer service. There were many executives from the Ace corporate offices and dozens and dozens of retailers who made themselves available for interviews and visits. There are two gentlemen I want to single out for their extraordinary—dare I say amazing—efforts to help bring this book to life. Tom Knox and Jay Heubner. Thank you, gentlemen! This project would not have happened without you.

Finally, I want to acknowledge and thank my family, which includes my wife, Cindy, my son, Brian, and my daughters, Alex and Casey. I'm lucky to have a family that puts up with my crazy schedule and time-consuming projects. They enthusiastically support me in all of my endeavors. I appreciate and love them for that—and much more. The kids are getting older and we have just one left at home. Whenever we are all together, usually for a holiday or a family trip, it is a very special time. I never realized just how much I would cherish those times. And just like a good book, I look forward to our next chapter.

INDEX

A

Accountability of customer's experience, 150–152

Ace Hardware

Ace Rewards program at, 198

active evangelists for, 192–193

alignment at, 28–29

as under appreciated brand, 11

associates at, 24

checking with, 21–22

brand promises of, 21

as business-to-business brand, 15, 19

as business-to-consumer brand, 19

buyer behavior at, 10–11

Certified Ace Helpful at, 29

community surrounding, 175–176

company mantra at, 29

as competitive, 61, 71

competitive pricing at, 12

connecting the dots at, 105

consistency at, 20, 99

core attributes of experience at, 99

core best practices at, 190–191

core standards driving, 14

as corporate rock star, 20

creating quality conversations with customers, 134

Customer Coordinator at, 201

customer feedback at, 181

as customer-focused business, 15

customer-focused culture of, 14, 17

customer satisfaction and, 10–11, 16

customer service at, 11, 16

easy way out and, 83–84

efforts to learn from customers, 53–54

as employee-centric business, 27, 41–42

e-newsletter of, 198

first impression tactic at, 132

Five-Dollar Lifeboat at, 31, 32

focusing on customers at, 127–128

giving back to the community, 214–216

as global company, 15, 19, 208–209

Good Samaritan stories at, 128–129

Helpful 101 certification at, 29

Helpful Index at, 29

helpfulness as mantra at, 21–23, 30–34, 80–81, 99, 139

hiring policies at, 105

importance of people, 20, 23

as individualized, 99

in-store decorations in, 209

as locally owned and operated, 10, 12, 15, 19, 204

managing the wait at, 163

money spent on advertising, 16

as network of privately owned stores, 16

number of stores, 10

operationalization of culture, 165–166

operation of, by independent business owners, 14

passion to serve and, 23–24

position of, 23

predictability at, 20

pride of store owners and, 21

product quality at, 10–11

profitability of, 24–25

putting people first at, 214–216

quality conversations with customers at, 134

reciprocity and, 204

revenue growth at, 16

as role model, 4

showing gratitude to customers of, 186–187

store owners and, 24–25

success of, 14, 19

tribal narratives from, 108

trust at, 99

use of mystery shoppers, 181

writing book about, 7

ABOUT THE AUTHOR

SHEP HYKEN is the founder and Chief Amazement Officer at Shepard Presentations, where he helps companies build loyal relationships with their customers and employees. He is a customer service and experience expert, an award-winning speaker, and a *New York Times* and *Wall Street Journal* bestselling author.

His articles have appeared in hundreds of publications. He is the author of *Moments of Magic, The Loyal Customer, The Cult of the Customer, The Amazement Revolution,* and *Amaze Every Customer Every Time.* His wide variety of clients includes smaller companies with fewer than fifty employees to corporate giants such as AT&T, American Express, General Motors, IBM, Kraft, Marriott, Toyota, Verizon, and many more.

A prolific speaker well known for his content-rich, entertaining and high-energy presentations, Hyken has been inducted into the National Speakers Association's Hall of Fame for lifetime achievement.

Learn more about Shep Hyken's speaking programs, customer service training programs, and advisory services at www.Hyken.com.

Follow on Twitter: @Hyken

Like on Facebook: ShepHykenSpeaker

Connect on LinkedIn: www.linkedin.com/in/ShepHyken

Join on Google +: www.gplus.to/ShepHyken

Watch on YouTube: www.YouTube.com/ShepHyken